The Prostate Cancer Treatment Book

Advice from leading prostate experts from the nation's top medical institutions

The Prostate Cancer Treatment Book

PETER D. GRIMM, D.O., JOHN C. BLASKO, M.D., and JOHN E. SYLVESTER, M.D.

Foreword by E. David Crawford, M.D., Professor of Surgery and Radiation Oncology,
University of Colorado Health Sciences Center

McGraw·Hill

New York   Chicago   San Francisco   Lisbon   London   Madrid   Mexico City
Milan   New Delhi   San Juan   Seoul   Singapore   Sydney   Toronto

The McGraw·Hill Companies

Library of Congress Cataloging-in-Publication Data

The prostate cancer treatment book / edited by Peter D. Grimm, John C. Blasko, John E. Sylvester.
     p.   cm.
Includes bibliographical references and index.
ISBN 0-07-142256-0
    1. Prostate—Cancer—Popular works.   I. Grimm, Peter D.   II. Blasko, John C.
III. Sylvester, John E.

RC280.P7P75993   2003
616.99'463—dc21   2003012684

The purpose of this book is to educate. It is sold with the understanding that the author and publisher shall have neither liability nor responsibility for any injury caused or alleged to be caused directly or indirectly by the information contained in this book. While strong efforts have been made to ensure its accuracy, the book's contents should not be construed as medical advice. Each person's health needs are unique. To obtain recommendations appropriate to your particular situation, please consult a qualified health care provider.

2 3 4 5 6 7 8 9 0   AGM/AGM   2 1 0 9 8 7 6 5 4

ISBN 0-07-142256-0

Interior illustrations: pages 4, 6, 7, 18, 45, 46, 48, 76, 77, 79, 96, 125, 130 by Jillian O'Malley. Pages 40, 56, 57, 58, 95, 117, 122, 163 by Tom Hodgson. Page 135 courtesy of The Seattle Prostate Institute.

McGraw-Hill books are available at special quantity discounts to use as premiums and sales promotions, or for use in corporate training programs. For more information, please write to the Director of Special Sales, Professional Publishing, McGraw-Hill, Two Penn Plaza, New York, NY 10121-2298. Or contact your local bookstore.

This book is printed on acid-free paper.

Contents

Part I The Foundation

Part II Treatment Options

Part III   Other Important Considerations

Foreword

PROSTATE CANCER BECAME the most commonly diagnosed male cancer in 1989, surpassing lung cancer in incidence. During that time, there was little in the way of public awareness of the disease and, unfortunately, most cases that were diagnosed were either locally advanced or metastatic to bone. Treatment was directed to control the disease through various types of hormonal therapies.

Efforts began in the early 1990s to inform men about prostate cancer and encourage early diagnosis. The good news is that the majority of cancers diagnosed this year will be localized, and the even better news is that many treatment options are available for men who have a localized cancer.

But, the plethora of treatment options presents a challenge and can represent a real dilemma. There is a perception that if you seek an opinion from surgeons, they recommend radical prostatectomy, but if you seek an opinion from radiation oncologists, the answer is radiation. Also, there may even be unreasonable expectations from treatment modalities. It is important for men to recognize that no treatment is going to make them a better man than they are now, and each treatment has a downside. To undergo treatment means they are trading the downside for the cure.

Because of all the changes in prostate cancer diagnosis, staging, and treatment, there is a lot of new information forthcoming each day. There are many sources of information: websites, brochures, books, magazines, and others. Many are not balanced and, in fact, are dangerous.

For *The Prostate Cancer Treatment Book*, Drs. Grimm, Blasko, and Sylvester have assembled the real leaders in the field of prostate cancer to provide a patient-friendly approach to understanding the diagnosis, staging, and treatments. This book contains a wealth of new and practical information. It provides a balanced view of various types of radiation and surgical approaches. The format of the book is unique and innovative. All of us who deal with men diagnosed with prostate cancer are cognizant of the many questions they have about the disease. By utilizing the question-and-answer approach, the editors provide a patient-friendly mechanism to educate men and their significant others about this disease.

I applaud this outstanding educational endeavor. This book is a must for all men who desire to educate themselves and their families about prostate cancer.

E. David Crawford, M.D.
Professor of Surgery and Radiation Oncology
University of Colorado Health Sciences Center
Denver, CO

Acknowledgments

THIS BOOK IS a collective effort of many men and women, each of whom has played an important role in its creation. Without the support of the following foundations, corporations, and individuals, *The Prostate Cancer Treatment Book* would still be only an idea: the Val A. Browning Foundation, Lee and Joan Thomas, the Kohlberg Foundation, Oncura (an Amersham Corporation), AstraZeneca, Imagyn Medical Technologies, Theragenics, Swedish Medical Center, Pfizer, Pro-Qura, and Rudolph Wolfe.

Nor would this book be possible without the cooperation and assistance of the following physicians: David C. Beyer, M.D., Arizona Oncology Services; Daniel H. Clarke, M.D., Inova Alexandria Cancer Center; E. David Crawford, M.D., University of Colorado Health Sciences Center; Brian J. Davis, M.D., Ph.D., Mayo Clinic; Jay L. Friedland, M.D., University Community Hospital; Celestia S. Higano, M.D., University of Washington; Deborah A. Kuban, M.D., M. D. Anderson Cancer Center; Gregory S. Merrick, M.D., Schiffler Cancer Center, Wheeling Hospital, and Wheeling Jesuit University; Jeff M. Michalski, M.D., Washington University School of Medicine; Brian J. Moran, M.D., Chicago Prostate Cancer Center; Mark A. Moyad, M.D., M.P.H., University of Michigan Medical Center; John P. Mulhall, M.D., Weill Medical College of Cornell University, New York Presbyterian Hospital, and Memorial Sloan-Kettering Cancer Center; Bradley R. Prestidge, M.D., Texas Prostate Brachytherapy Services; Mack Roach III, M.D., University of California, San Francisco;

Katsuto Shinohara, M.D., University of California, San Francisco; Ian M. Thompson, M.D., University of Texas Health Science Center at San Antonio; J. Brantley Thrasher, M.D., University of Kansas Medical Center; Kent Wallner, M.D., University of Washington; and Anthony L. Zietman, M.D., Harvard Medical School.

Also pivotal to this book's development were Swedish Medical Center's President and CEO Richard Peterson, Chief Operating Officer Cal Knight, and Vice President of Business Development Richard Keck. Swedish Cancer Institute Executive Director Albert Einstein Jr., M.D., and Swedish Medical Center Foundation Interim Executive Director Jon B. Olson were also instrumental.

We would be remiss if we did not acknowledge the men and their mates who courageously and openly shared the stories featured in this book, as well as the many men who contributed questions.

Also, special thanks to this book's writer, Maribeth Stephens; Judith McCarthy at McGraw-Hill for her editorial excellence; Jillian O'Malley for the wonderful illustrations; and Tom Hodgson for the clear, concise graphics. Hats off to everyone at the Seattle Prostate Institute (SPI) and Pro-Qura, with specific thanks to SPI's Charles Heaney, Deanna Jacobsen, Sheila Kaufman, R.N., Jan Rose, Alea Sando, R.N., and Mary Schotanus, as well as Pro-Qura's Lori Holmes, Lisa Yoshizumi, Mike Sitter, and Jennifer Bates. We would also like to thank Robert Parker, M.D., our mentor.

While not involved in this book, there is one more physician we would like to thank, as well. Many years ago, Dr. Haakon Ragde brought knowledge of ultrasound-guided prostate brachytherapy to the United States from Europe. We appreciate his contribution during the formative years of today's modern seed implant procedure.

Introduction

Peter D. Grimm, D.O.; John C. Blasko, M.D.;
John E. Sylvester, M.D.

"YOU HAVE PROSTATE cancer." Those words can shift the axis of your world. You may feel as if your body is betraying you. You might ask, "How can this happen to me? Why has my body revolted? What should I do?"

After the initial shock subsides, your attention likely switches from wondering *why* you ended up with cancer to *how* to fight it. You may approach the cancer as if a beast has invaded your body and conquering it requires only finding the right treatment. Like many others in the growing army of prostate cancer patients, you scour medical journals, seek second and third opinions, and gather data from the Internet.

You quickly learn that what you *thought* was a direct path into battle is really a labyrinth of more questions, second opinions, hard-to-pronounce medical terminology, and even harder-to-read lab reports. You may even receive conflicting recommendations from professionals, not to mention potentially confusing advice from family and friends.

Your task would be easy if only one treatment existed. But there's a myriad: watchful waiting, surgery, hormonal therapy, external beam radiation, and radioactive seed implantation. And that's just the beginning. There are different kinds of external beam radiation, varying ways of

xiii

implanting radioactive seeds, and alternate methods of removing the prostate. Now mix in the possibility of combined treatments (hormonal therapy plus radiation, for example) and you have even more to sort through. No wonder it's confusing!

We understand this frustration. That's why we wrote *The Prostate Cancer Treatment Book*. This is the only question-and-answer book in which numerous prostate cancer experts answer the very questions *you* are asking.

How do we know what you're asking? We see men like you in our offices every day, searching for the treatment that's right for them. Besides gathering questions from our own medical practices, we also asked men in prostate cancer support groups to send us their questions. Specifically, we invited them to share their inquiries about what they wished they had asked their doctors early on. Next, we sent these hundreds of questions to well-known prostate cancer experts in urology, radiation oncology, medical oncology, and nutrition at some of the most prestigious medical institutions in the United States—M. D. Anderson Cancer Center, Mayo Clinic, Memorial Sloan-Kettering Cancer Center, and University of California, San Francisco—to name just a few. This book is the result. Distilled in these pages is the wisdom of men who've battled prostate cancer and doctors from world-class institutions who've treated tens of thousands of patients from all over the world.

How to Use This Book

The physicians who contributed to this volume hope to spare you and your family from spending an inordinate amount of time and energy collecting and organizing information. While we encourage you to read other available literature and talk to your own doctor, we believe this book is one of the best places to begin learning about prostate cancer and understanding treatment options. We devote many pages to seed implantation, yet provide considerable information about other treatments so you and your doctor can make the choice that's best for you. By the time you finish reading this volume, we anticipate you will have a greater understanding of:

- The prostate and its function
- Dietary changes and supplemental remedies effective for overall prostate health
- What to expect during common screening tests, and what to anticipate if doctors recommend additional tests
- The positives and negatives of commonly recommended prostate cancer treatments
- The best candidates for seed implantation, how doctors perform the implant, and the scientific evidence showing long-term effectiveness and side effects
- What questions to ask your doctors
- Where you and your mate can go for support and more information

Each chapter starts with a short introduction followed by several pages of questions and answers. Since each chapter focuses on a particular topic, you can peruse only those chapters most important to you or read the book straight through. We also have included stories of real patients, how they reacted to learning they had prostate cancer, how they researched their treatment options, what they went through during and after treatment, and how they're doing now. Note that their stories are true, but the names we use are not.

Prostate cancer is a battle. It is our desire that this book becomes a valuable tool in the entire arsenal that you and your family use to attack—and ultimately conquer—this disease.

Part I

THE FOUNDATION

I

What Good Is a Prostate, Anyway?

Ian M. Thompson, M.D.; J. Brantley Thrasher, M.D.;
Mark A. Moyad, M.D., M.P.H.; John E. Sylvester, M.D.

MOST PEOPLE RARELY—if ever—think about the prostate gland. They understand it's a male organ in the pelvic area, situated somewhere between the navel and testicles. They may be vaguely aware that it serves some purpose related to creating offspring. And they know that measuring the prostate specific antigen (PSA) level is an important annual blood test for many men. But the gland is tucked deep inside and it rarely causes trouble, so there's little incentive to take the time to learn about it.

But when the words *prostate cancer* are uttered, suddenly the prostate leaps to the forefront of consciousness and the race is on to gather as much information as possible, in as little time as possible.

So, that's where we begin. Chapter 1 helps you clear this first hurdle in conquering prostate cancer by explaining what the prostate gland is, what it does, and what can go wrong with it.

The Prostate

What is the prostate and what function does it serve?

The prostate is a conglomeration of tiny glands, ducts, and muscle tissue encased by fibrous tissue. It produces fluid that contains hormones and proteins to keep sperm alive after ejaculation as the sperm searches for an egg to fertilize.

The average size of a prostate is about 30 to 40 grams, about the size of a small lime or walnut. Its texture is firm. About one-third of the prostate is composed of muscular tissue, with the rest being glandular tissue.

As a man ages, his prostate often gets bigger, sometimes doubling or tripling in size. Although there is a lot of discussion about prostate enlargement in aging men and the uncomfortable symptoms that this can cause, it's important to remember that not all men experience prostate enlargement, and cancer is not responsible for this enlargement.

The prostate's zones include the transition, the central, the anterior, and the peripheral (see Figure 1.1).

The transition zone is the most interior part of the prostate; it immediately surrounds the urethra (the slender tube that carries urine away from

---

FIGURE 1.1   The Prostate

The prostate zones include the transition zone, the central zone, the anterior zone, and the peripheral zone, which is closest to the rectum. The peripheral zone is the area where prostate cancer most often occurs.

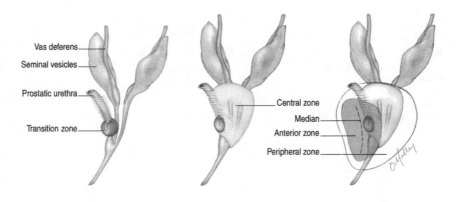

---

the bladder and out of the body through the tip of the penis). The transition zone can begin to grow after age 40, with this noncancerous enlargement possibly leading to urinary difficulties.

The central zone is up near the bladder and is the seat of about one-third of the glands that make and secrete prostatic fluid. The central zone, similar to the transition zone, is generally the part of the prostate that grows after a man turns 40. Prostate cancer is unusual in the central zone and if it does develop, it tends to be a slower growing type of cancer.

The anterior zone (*anterior* means "front") is mostly muscle tissue. The peripheral zone is at the back of the gland and is the portion closest to the rectum. It contains most of the secretion-producing glands and is where prostate cancer usually develops.

Are there "right" and "left" glands, or are there "right" and "left" sides of one gland?

Physicians describe a right side and a left side, but in reality there is only a subtle demarcation between the two sides. Think of a plum. It's one fruit, but the small groove down the middle leaves the impression of two halves. That's similar to the prostate gland.

Where is the prostate, and what other important organs are near it?

If you measured how far the prostate is situated inside the pelvic area, it's about two inches from the perineum, which is the region of exterior skin and internal muscle between the anus and the scrotum. The gland sits just below the bladder and in front of the rectum (see Figure 1.2). Off the base of the prostate and behind the bladder are the two seminal vesicles, which produce most of the fluid that makes up the ejaculate.

What are the apex and the base of the prostate?

The base of the prostate is the wider part of the gland that nestles up to the bladder. The apex is the more pointed end of the gland that faces down toward the perineum.

How does the prostate work?

Just before ejaculation, sperm from the testicles is transported into the urethra by a long tube called the vas deferens. This sperm combines with fluid both from the seminal vesicles and the prostate, creating semen. The

FIGURE 1.2   Organs Near the Prostate

The prostate is in front of the rectum and below the bladder. The urethra, which is the slender tube carrying urine from the bladder and out the tip of the penis, runs through the middle of the prostate.

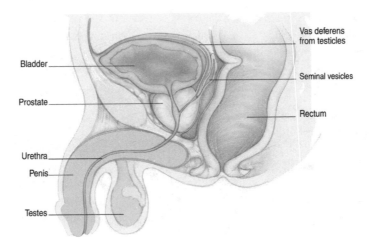

prostate and adjacent muscular contractions then propel the semen out of the urethra through the tip of the penis for ejaculation.

BPH and Prostatis

What is benign prostatic hyperplasia (BPH) and what causes it?

Benign prostatic hyperplasia is the medical term for noncancerous enlargement of the prostate. At about age 40, the transition and/or central portion of the prostate can begin to grow. As one or both of these areas enlarge, the growth can compress the part of the urethra that runs through the prostate (see Figure 1.3).

The prostate is sensitive to the normal male hormones (androgens) inside a man's body. The primary androgen, of course, is testosterone, and it's testosterone that seems to be partially responsible for BPH in older men.

FIGURE 1.3 Benign Prostatic Hyperplasia (BPH)

As a man ages, interior portions of his prostate may grow and choke off the urethra, causing urinary problems. This noncancerous growth is called BPH.

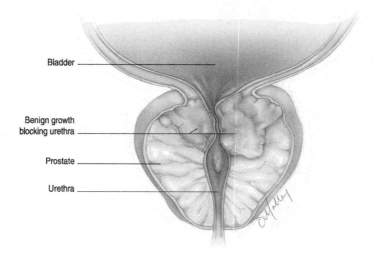

Bladder

Benign growth blocking urethra

Prostate

Urethra

What are the symptoms of BPH?

Depending on how the prostatic tissue grows, it may cause different symptoms in different men. However, the usual symptoms are more frequent urination, especially in the middle of the night. Also, the bladder may not feel completely empty, or there may be a need to push or strain because of a slow urinary stream. Another possible symptom is urgency (meaning a strong desire to urinate). Urgency occurs when the bladder gets the signal that it's full. If this is a very strong signal and a man cannot relieve himself quickly, it's possible to leak urine.

Is treatment of BPH always necessary?

No, not always. In fact, many men with BPH aren't bothered by symptoms at all. It could be that the onset of symptoms is so gradual or the symptoms are so minor that they don't adversely impact quality of life. For instance, a man may have to get up just once or twice a night and urinate only a bit more frequently during the day.

When symptoms progress to a point of interfering with usual daily activities—such as a man being unable to take a long car trip because he has to use a restroom frequently or he gets out of bed several times at night—then he'll probably seek treatment.

Can drugs treat BPH?

Yes. The three classes of medications most frequently used to treat BPH are alpha-blockers, 5-alpha-reductase inhibitors, and herbal supplements.

- **Alpha-blockers.** These medications relax the smooth muscle tissue at the neck of the bladder and in the prostate, to let patients urinate more freely. These medications are very effective in improving symptoms, usually within days to weeks. Alpha-blockers are generally safe but sometimes can make patients dizzy or weak. Some alpha-blockers may also cause a slight decrease in blood pressure. A few patients can't take alpha-blockers because the drugs leave them feeling fatigued and drained.

- **5-alpha-reductase inhibitors.** Finasteride (Proscar) and dutasteride (Avodart) are approved in the United States to treat BPH. These drugs block the conversion of testosterone into the more potent dihydrotestosterone. Used over three to six months, 5-alpha-reductase inhibitors shrink the prostate. In large clinical trials, the men who took these medications were more likely to have an improvement in urinary symptoms.

  These medications appear to be safe but can be associated with swelling or tenderness of the breasts, difficulty with erections, decreased sexual drive, or decreased ejaculate volume. On the flip side, one of the advantages of 5-alpha-reductase inhibitors is that they grow hair. In fact, the Food and Drug Administration has approved finasteride for men who have male pattern baldness.

- **Herbal supplements.** Many herbal supplements are used around the world to alleviate BPH symptoms. Three common herbal agents are saw palmetto, Pygeum africanum, and Cernilton. Some clinical trials have suggested some effectiveness of these agents. A collaboration is under development by the National Institutes of Health to determine their effectiveness compared to placebo.

What's All the Excitement About Herbal Supplements?

Many men take herbal remedies touted to alleviate BPH symptoms. Here's a quick rundown of three of the most popular. Word to the wise: before you take *any* supplement, talk with your doctor. (For more information on supplements and prostate cancer, turn to Chapter 2.)

Saw Palmetto

This dwarf palm tree is native to the southeastern United States and the West Indies. The capsule from your local health food or grocery store is made of the plant's berries. In other preparations, fresh berries are soaked in water to create a kind of tea.

The *Journal of the American Medical Association* (JAMA) published a review of nearly 20 studies on saw palmetto conducted during the last three decades.[1] The JAMA article concluded that saw palmetto (320 mg per day) showed improvements in urinary symptoms similar to improvements seen in men who took finasteride to relieve BPH symptoms. But most of these studies were of short duration and included only small numbers of men. Additional research is needed to determine saw palmetto's effectiveness over the long term. In general, however, saw palmetto appears to be an acceptable choice to help with the symptoms of BPH.

A dosage of 320 mg per day (or 160 mg twice a day) appears to be effective in some men in decreasing BPH symptoms, but it can take up to six weeks for results to show up. There's no evidence, good or bad, that saw palmetto has any effect on prostate cancer; it has not been studied for this condition. Also, note that a very small percentage of men, about 1 percent, will experience erectile dysfunction as a side effect of taking saw palmetto.

Pygeum Africanum

The common name for this tree is the African plum tree. It's an evergreen tree that grows all across the African continent at altitudes of 3,000 feet or higher. As far back as the eighteenth century, European travelers learned from South African tribes how to use the bark of this tree to soothe men's urinary symptoms. Today, this preparation is used widely on the European continent. In the United States, few studies have been conducted as to its effectiveness to relieve BPH symptoms. The usual dosage in Europe is 50 mg to 100 mg, two times daily.

Cernilton

This is the commercial name of a product that is the extract of several kinds of rye grass pollens. It claims to be an anti-inflammatory and to relax the muscles that surround the urethra. Men take it to help with chronic nonbacterial prostatitis, although science can't explain exactly how it works—perhaps it inhibits an enzyme that leads to prostate inflammation. The common dosage is 63 mg to 126 mg, two or three times per day. Some men experience upset stomach or heartburn with this preparation.

A Final Thought

It is unclear whether or to what degree any of these herbal supplements affect urinary symptoms or prostate health. Because of the negligible oversight of the sale of many of these supplements, it is wise to ask your physician whether these supplements are right for you.

Are there surgical treatments for BPH?

Generally, doctors reserve surgery for men whose BPH symptoms don't respond to medications, who are unable tolerate medication's side effects, or who develop serious problems that medication can't control, such as the inability to urinate, kidney complications, or urinary infections.

The most common surgical treatment for BPH is a transurethral resection of the prostate—TURP. In this procedure, a urologist inserts a surgical instrument through the urethra into the prostate. The instrument uses a tiny loop to remove tissue. An electrical current runs through the loop and the surgeon cuts out the obstructing tissue in small chips. The chips are flushed out and a catheter remains in place for a time. Once the catheter is removed, this wider channel becomes the new urinary passage out of the bladder.

A TURP requires an anesthetic and is generally either same-day surgery or requires only an overnight stay. If a prostate is too large to be treated via a TURP, surgeons may remove the obstructing part of the gland completely, either by making an incision through the abdomen or through the perineum.

Less invasive treatments are also available. These therapies involve heating or freezing the prostate, laser treatment, microwave treatment, or the use of radio waves. The idea behind all of them is to relieve pressure on the urethra by destroying a portion of the enlarged prostate tissue and letting the body reabsorb the tissue over time. In general, these treatments have not been around as long as most current medical and surgical treatments, so there's little long-term data about their effectiveness and side effects. Initial results suggest that while they are not as effective as a TURP, they do significantly improve urinary symptoms.

What are the side effects of BPH surgery?

Side effects can include bleeding, infection, urinary leakage, or a narrowing of the urinary channel due to scar tissue (stricture) that can result in a urinary blockage. It's also possible that despite the TURP, symptoms won't improve. Then there's the risk of retrograde ejaculation—the ejaculate going into the bladder instead of coming out of the urethra. For younger men who still desire to father children, this is a problem.

What is prostatitis, what causes it, and how is it treated?

Prostatitis is an inflammation of the prostate. Similar to BPH, prostatitis can mean uncomfortable symptoms such as urinary frequency or urgency. Other symptoms may be fever and chills, difficulty in urination, pain in the region below the scrotum (perineal pain), low-back pain, joint or muscle pain, a tender or swollen prostate, or painful ejaculation.

There are three types of prostatitis: acute bacterial prostatitis, chronic bacterial prostatitis, and nonbacterial prostatitis.

- **Acute bacterial prostatitis.** Acute bacterial prostatitis is the easiest to diagnose because its symptoms—problems with urination, fever, and pain—come on so fast. However, doctors have a murky understanding of how bacterial prostatitis develops. We know it comes from bacteria. But where all the bacteria come from is less clear. Sometimes, the bacteria come from urine that has pooled in the bladder. If the bladder cannot empty itself, the remaining urine provides a supportive environment for bacterial growth. The usual treatment for acute bacterial prostatitis is a course of antibiotics.

- **Chronic bacterial prostatitis.** Bacteria also cause this, but the symptoms are typically less severe than acute bacterial prostatitis. In some men, the only symptoms of chronic bacterial prostatitis may be recurrent bladder infections.

  Antibiotics are also called for in treating chronic bacterial prostatitis, but it could take up to a month or even longer to knock out the infection.

- **Nonbacterial prostatitis.** Physicians don't know what causes this form of prostatitis. Because the cause is a mystery, a patient may have to undergo a series of treatments to relieve symptoms. Often the first step is to prescribe antibiotics in case there's an infectious organism in the prostate. If antibiotics fail, a variety of drugs including alpha-blockers or 5-alpha-reductase inhibitors may be tried. Herbal therapies, as for BPH, have been found to be helpful in some patients. In a few cases, physicians have used radio frequency or microwaves to treat chronic prostatitis. These treatments have some success at relieving symptoms, but it's too early to say which of these treatments will provide the best long-term relief.

Can I do anything to reduce the discomfort from prostatitis?
Some men suffering from prostatitis can reduce their symptoms by avoiding caffeine—coffee, chocolate, cola, and the like. Strong spices tend to further irritate an inflamed prostate, so it's valuable to avoid those, too. For some patients, alcohol can make symptoms worse, so these men make a point of not drinking anything containing alcohol.

Does prostatitis or BPH cause prostate cancer?
There's no convincing proof at this time that these conditions are related to prostate cancer. There is some developing evidence that suggests that inflammation *may* be related to prostate cancer but this information is in its very early stages and may prove to be incorrect. There is nothing yet definitively linking a man with a history of prostatitis or BPH to a greater chance of

developing prostate cancer. However, it is interesting that some of the most promising prostate cancer prevention drugs may be the ones that already help men with BPH, or in some cases, prostatitis.

Can I tell without diagnostic tests if my symptoms are BPH, prostatitis, or prostate cancer?

Prostate cancer usually does not cause symptoms. For this reason, *usually* (but not always) urinary symptoms are not related to prostate cancer. However, BPH and prostate cancer can co-exist. That's why if you have any urinary symptoms at all, you need to see your doctor. Only a good medical and urologic history, a urine culture, and a thorough examination can best determine what's going on.

Prostate Cancer

What is prostate cancer?

Prostate cancer is an uncontrolled growth of cells that line the ducts of the prostate gland. These abnormal cells can spread throughout the prostate and nearby organs, such as the seminal vesicles. If not caught early, they can spread (metastasize) to other regions of the body through the lymph or blood systems.

Do different types of cancer appear in the prostate?

Most of the time when doctors talk about prostate cancer, they're referring to adenocarcinoma. This cancer arises from the cells of the prostate's ducts.

However, there are a few other rare cancers in the prostate. One is urothelial cell carcinoma (UCC). Urothelial cell carcinoma originates from the layer of cells that line the inside of the urethra and the bladder. This tumor is frequently seen in association with bladder cancer.

An extremely rare cancer of the prostate is a sarcoma. A sarcoma originates from the muscular and connective tissue in the prostate and is treated quite differently.

Who's most likely to develop prostate cancer?

The possibility of developing prostate cancer increases after the age of 50; about 70 percent of all prostate cancers are diagnosed in men older than 65.

Approximately 180,000 to 200,000 men per year develop prostate cancer in the United States. It's the second leading cause of cancer death in men, only behind lung cancer. There is some good news, however, to report about prostate cancer. Since 1991, the risk of prostate cancer death has decreased by 20 percent.

Unlike lung cancer, which can be attributed to preventable risk factors such as smoking, prostate cancer risk factors—age, family history, and race—obviously are not preventable.

- **Age and family history.** Many men develop prostate cancer as they age. In studies of older men whose prostates were examined after they died, many had prostate cancer at the time of their death. However, most of these men didn't die *of* prostate cancer, they died *with* prostate cancer. Most of these men succumbed to other health conditions and just happened to have prostate cancer when they died.

  The second predominant risk factor is family history. An average American man has a one in six chance of being diagnosed with prostate cancer during his lifetime. But if his father or brother (these are first-degree relatives) has prostate cancer, his risk doubles. The risk goes even higher if two or more first-degree relatives (a brother *and* the father) have prostate cancer.

  The age at which the first-degree relative is diagnosed with prostate cancer is an essential factor in predicting risk. If a man's first-degree relative is diagnosed at a young age—under the age of 55—the risk that his sons or brothers will develop prostate cancer is significantly greater, possibly due to genetic factors.

  If a first-degree relative is diagnosed with prostate cancer much later in life, say at age 80, there is less chance that other men in his family will have a strong genetic tendency to develop it.

- **Race.** The third risk factor is race. African-Americans not only have a higher risk of developing prostate cancer, they are also more likely to develop prostate cancer at an earlier age. No one is sure why African-American men are more prone to prostate cancer. Perhaps it's because African-American men in general have less access to health care due to socioeconomic factors. Perhaps it's diet. Perhaps it's genetics. Perhaps it's a combination of these and other factors.

Some evidence points to hormones, especially male hormones, as being the cause for greater risk in this population. African-American men have been found to have higher levels of testosterone before the age of 40 (but there are no consistent findings for higher testosterone for African-Americans older than 40). Whether African-American men are also diagnosed with more aggressive prostate cancer is uncertain and controversial. However, what is certain and not as controversial is the fact that African-American men have a higher risk of being diagnosed earlier with this disease.

There's no doubt that men in Asian nations have a low risk of prostate cancer. Yet for Asians who immigrate to the United States, within one or two generations the men's risk of developing prostate cancer climbs to almost as high as that for the average white American male. Again, no one is sure why. The theory most often offered is the significant change in diet and lifestyle. In fact, some researchers have found that higher rates of prostate cancer are now showing up in cities such as Tokyo, where diets and lifestyles are becoming more westernized.

There are a number of additional theories on why prostate cancer develops—environmental risks and a genetic link. All of these theories are being intensely researched but no final answers are yet available.

Are there substances found naturally in the body that can stimulate prostate cancer growth?

We've already touched upon how testosterone fuels prostate cancer. Human growth factors, too, may play a role in prostate cancer development, and they are now being closely researched.

As the human body grows to its full size, it secretes growth factors. Similarly, when adults experience weight gain (especially rapid weight gain) their bodies also secrete high levels of growth factors. In laboratory tests, these growth factors seem to stimulate the growth of prostate cancer and may be related to more aggressive cancers, which is why physicians are concerned about overweight men who have an increased risk of prostate cancer.

If I take testosterone, am I at greater risk of developing prostate cancer?

Testosterone therapy is an important form of treatment for a number of conditions. Because prostate cancer is sensitive to testosterone, taking it *may* increase the risk of developing the disease. Fortunately in most cases, if prostate cancer develops when a man is taking testosterone, it does not appear to be different from other prostate cancers and it should respond to treatment. If you truly qualify for testosterone treatment, you should get regular blood tests to measure your PSA level and have regular prostate exams. Also, if you are diagnosed with prostate cancer, it is currently not a good idea to start or continue taking testosterone.

If I take dehydroepiandrosterone (DHEA), am I at increased risk for prostate cancer?

Dehydroepiandrosterone (DHEA) is an adrenal gland hormone. Because DHEA levels are highest in puberty and young adulthood, some call DHEA the anti-aging drug.

Studies show that in men with *normal* testosterone levels, DHEA supplements don't increase testosterone. In fact, they can significantly increase estrogen levels (estrogen is a hormone that aids in the development of female body characteristics). In addition, DHEA can cause a drop in high-density lipoprotein, or HDL, which is the good kind of cholesterol the body needs.

For men with *subnormal* testosterone levels, DHEA does tend to increase the testosterone level. But it also increases estrogen and could influence the risk of developing cardiovascular disease.

Ask your doctor if any of the dietary supplements you are interested in taking are hormone precursors. Many of the so-called "sex enhancement" supplements sold today may increase testosterone levels. Large doses of DHEA or other so-called hormone precursors such as androstenedione (also known as andro) may complicate prostate cancer. Our advice is that any man concerned about his testosterone level should work with his physician. Although DHEA is widely available, it should be closely monitored by a physician who has special expertise in male hormone replacement.

How fast does prostate cancer grow?

Compared to most other kinds of cancer, prostate adenocarcinoma is *usually* very slow-growing. It can begin at a relatively early age, possibly in the 30s or 40s. Because it grows so slowly, it's not usually diagnosed until after age 55 to 60. In some situations, though, the cancer will grow and spread very fast.

How will a doctor know if my cancer is fast-growing?

There are several ways to predict the tumor's speed of growth. The first is to watch how fast the PSA level is rising; this is called PSA velocity. Another measure is the Gleason score. The higher the Gleason score, the more aggressive the cancer. (PSA velocity and the Gleason score are discussed in detail in Chapter 3.) A final method involves repeated physical examination or radiology studies (such as an MRI or bone scans) to monitor growth of the cancer.

If prostate cancer spreads outside the gland, where does it typically spread?

Prostate cancer can spread in several ways. It usually spreads first through the capsule of the prostate. This spread outside the gland is often only a few millimeters. It can also move into the seminal vesicles. Spread to the seminal vesicles is seen less often these days, probably because the disease is being caught earlier.

Prostate cancer can occasionally spread to other parts of the body. Cancer cells can enter the lymphatic vessels around the prostate and then spread to the lymph nodes in the pelvis (see Figure 1.4). Another way prostate cancer spreads is through the bloodstream.

Ultimately, cancer cells that enter the lymph channels can spread, through the blood, to almost any organ in the body. Because of what seem to be special growth factors, the prostate cancer cells have an affinity for growing in bone—often the bones of the spine, pelvis, or long bones, such as the femur (upper leg) or humerus (upper arm).

To determine if prostate cancer has spread to the bone, a bone scan is performed in some prostate cancer patients. If prostate cancer cells begin to grow in the bones, it's still called prostate cancer (not bone cancer) and may be treated with hormonal and radiation therapies.

Can a biopsy cause cancer cells to spread from the prostate to the rest of the body?

There is no reliable evidence to suggest that a transrectal biopsy causes cancer cells to spread to the rest of the body. In addition, keep in mind that a biopsy is the best possible way to diagnose prostate cancer.

FIGURE 1.4   Pelvic Lymph Nodes

One of the ways cancer can spread is by entering the nearby lymphatic vessels and migrating to the lymph nodes around the pelvis and beyond.

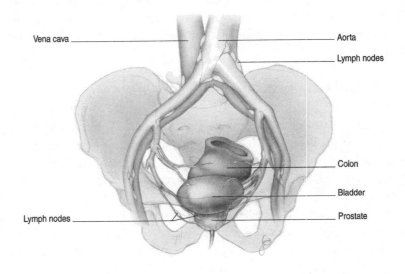

How often is advanced prostate cancer seen in first-time patients?

Prior to the PSA screening era, approximately 30 percent of patients came in with advanced disease at initial presentation. Years ago, some prostate cancer patients had never seen a doctor until serious urinary symptoms forced a visit to a physician. Unfortunately, many of these patients had advanced prostate cancer at the time of diagnosis. Today, in areas where PSA screening is used, less than 6 percent of newly diagnosed prostate cancer patients have widespread cancer.

Since most men develop prostate cancer, why can't I just have the gland removed before it shows up in me?

It's true that the prostate is not a vital organ like the heart or liver. Its primary purpose is to help keep sperm alive so human beings can reproduce.

The prostate *is* valuable in that it supports several structures important for ejaculation—the urethra, vas deferens, and ejaculatory ducts.

However, some men who are at higher risk of developing prostate cancer and whose fathering years are behind them have, on occasion, asked their urologists to remove their prostates as a preventive measure. There are some serious problems with this line of thinking. First, we don't have very good ways to identify high-risk men at this time. While we know what risk factors have an impact, we would have a hard time telling which man *for sure* will get prostate cancer and, therefore, would truly benefit from prophylactic (preventive) treatment.

Radical prostatectomies (surgical removal of the prostate and surrounding tissues) can also cause unwanted side effects—impotence and incontinence being just two. It's entirely possible that a patient who had his prostate removed in hopes of preventing prostate cancer would never have developed the disease in the first place. Because screening helps catch prostate cancer in the earliest stage—and early stage disease usually has a good prognosis—the benefit of removing the prostate as a preventive measure must be weighed against the potential side effects.

2

How Is Heart Health Connected to Prostate Cancer Risk?

Mark A. Moyad, M.D., M.P.H.; Peter D. Grimm, D.O.

BACON CHEESEBURGER WITH extra cheddar or a chicken Caesar salad? Curly fries or a whole grain roll? Large soda or unsweetened iced tea? Will you watch reruns tonight or take a walk with your spouse?

By now, you can guess this chapter deals with diet and exercise. Tempted to skip it? Please don't. This chapter contains information about the most potent self-directed activities that can affect your overall health and response to prostate cancer treatment. Moreover, if you have brothers, sons, or other men in your immediate family who have not been diagnosed with prostate cancer, they will benefit from reading this chapter, too. The advice in the next few pages will do them a world of good for their overall health and could go a long way in possibly preventing prostate cancer.

The Placebo Effect

One note before we begin. Many men take over-the-counter supplements or follow a special diet as part of a health routine. In and of themselves, these activities are not bad. But to fully assess how well those supplements or that diet is working, be aware of something called the "placebo effect."

In clinical trials, researchers often observe that men and women who take a fake pill experience the same benefit as those who take the real drug. An example is a headache study in which a sugar pill (the placebo) is given to half of the participants and aspirin to the remaining subjects. The effect on the group that took the sugar pill is then compared to the effect on the group that took the aspirin. For some patients, the sugar pill relieves the headache just as well as the aspirin—this is what researchers call the placebo effect.

Scientists don't know why the placebo effect occurs, but they do know that a large proportion of patients—between 25 percent and 50 percent—taking dietary supplements experience it. That's why we recommend reading medical literature on any supplement before you take it. It can be difficult finding medical literature pertaining to supplements and their placebo effects because companies that manufacture supplements tend to report only positive studies. And the scientific papers casting doubt on supplements' effectiveness often are relegated to the last pages of obscure journals. Many book publishers are reluctant to publish negative reports, too.

The best sources for obtaining a balanced perspective of a supplement's effectiveness are medical journal reviews, which are articles assessing all of the studies to date about a particular topic.

Also, when perusing a medical journal article on supplements, be certain to review any editorial associated with the study you're reading. The journal's editors write these pieces for the sole purpose of questioning the authors' conclusions, and they may shed more light on the study itself.

A good example of how editorials benefit readers is in a recent trial looking at selenium. This study indicated that this mineral supplement was beneficial against cancer. When this news hit the popular press, lots of folks started taking selenium without question. But those who read the editorial in the same issue of the journal that ran the results of the selenium trial learned that not everyone benefited equally from selenium. Read on to learn the full story about whether selenium really might help prevent cancer for everyone, or if all the hoopla around selenium supplements is a simple misunderstanding.

Prevention and Supplements

What's the link between prostate cancer and a heart-healthy diet?

Keep this in mind: If it's heart-healthy, it's prostate-healthy. For anyone concerned about prostate cancer, a good rule of thumb is to look at what's happening in the world of cardiovascular disease. Ninety-nine times out of 100, what's good for the heart is good for the prostate.

What are the best supplements to prevent prostate cancer and in what quantity?

This is a difficult question. In a clinical trial at the University of Arizona, researchers had a large group of men and women consume 200 micrograms (mcg) of selenium per day for an average of four and a half years. The idea was to see if selenium could prevent skin cancer recurrence in the participants. At the end of the trial, researchers discovered a 37 percent decrease in overall cancer rates. For men, there was a 63 percent reduction in prostate cancer risk. This news helped turn the selenium supplement market into a billion-dollar industry.

While that trial seemed to indicate that selenium was a miracle pill to help prevent cancer, the truth of the matter is that the trial was looking at whether selenium could reduce the risk of skin cancer. There was *no* decreased risk of skin cancer. In fact, they found a slightly *higher* risk of skin cancer in those taking the selenium supplements!

The researchers also found that only those men who were *already* deficient in selenium benefited in terms of prostate cancer reduction. If a man started this trial with normal or high levels of selenium, there was no risk reduction of prostate cancer associated with taking the supplement. Plus, most of the people who benefited from the selenium supplements were smokers. Smokers are notoriously low in a number of natural antioxidants such as selenium.

Here's our take-home message: If you're deficient in selenium or if you're a smoker, you might benefit by taking a selenium supplement. But if neither of those is true, we believe that following a moderately healthy diet or taking an inexpensive multivitamin each day means you're probably already getting enough selenium.

What's the downside of getting too much selenium?

Selenium is a mineral that's deposited in soft tissue, so it's difficult for the body to get rid of excess amounts. Selenium toxicity or overdose leads to temporary or permanent loss of large clumps of hair and loss of fingernails, not to mention nausea, gastrointestinal problems, fatigue, and dizziness.

Will taking vitamin E supplements prevent prostate cancer?

Unfortunately, the benefit of vitamin E is similar to selenium in that it has only worked in smokers trying to prevent cancer. In the largest supplement study ever, researchers followed about 32,000 men (all smokers) who took a vitamin E supplement or a placebo. In the end, there appeared to be a 32 percent reduction in prostate cancer risk for those who took the vitamin E supplement. This made headlines in nearly every newspaper in the country.

The popular press, however, did not report that researchers also examined weight as a risk factor throughout the entire trial. The researchers found that obese men had a 40 percent increased risk of prostate cancer. It seems that the negative impact of carrying too much weight was greater than the positive impact of popping a vitamin E pill. But this aspect of the study failed to get into the public media.

Lifestyle changes potentially have a greater impact than taking any over-the-counter pills. We advise that unless you're a smoker, the benefits of taking supplemental vitamin E may be minimal.

Is there a difference between synthetic vitamin E and natural vitamin E?

Yes. The type of synthetic vitamin E found in many supplements is vastly different from the vitamin E found in food. Synthetic vitamin E is inexpensive to produce, and that's why it's generally inexpensive to purchase. It's the naturally occurring gamma form of vitamin E, found in the diet, that's been shown to be helpful in discouraging prostate cancer cell growth.

If you think taking synthetic vitamin E while eating a diet rich in natural vitamin E will give prostate cancer a double whammy, think again. Synthetic vitamin E prevents the body from absorbing natural vitamin E from food. So, synthetic vitamin E supplements may be interfering with the natural dietary vitamin E that helps fight prostate cancer.

You can purchase natural vitamin E supplements, but they tend to be expensive. These are labeled with "d"—d-gamma tocopherol or d-alpha tocopherol, for example. All *synthetic* sources of vitamin E are labeled with "dl," for instance, dl-gamma tocopherol or dl-alpha tocopherol.

We believe that you can do just as well by eating a diet rich in naturally occurring vitamin E. The best sources of dietary vitamin E are nuts, seeds, egg yolks, and the heart-healthy oils such as soybean, canola, and olive.

One final word about supplemental vitamin E. In the past several trials looking at vitamin E and heart disease, the subjects were told to take large amounts of vitamin E pills. But at the end of the study, heart vessel blockages showed little to no change. Therefore, the initial enthusiasm years ago for the *synthetic* vitamin E supplement, especially in the cardiovascular world, has really died down. But *dietary* vitamin E still holds some promise for benefit.

Do omega-3 fatty acids prevent prostate cancer?

Fatty acids are one of fat's raw materials. Omega-3 fatty acid is a type of polyunsaturated fat, and polyunsaturated fat appears to decrease the unhealthy fatty compounds in the blood, which is why they're so beneficial to cardiovascular health.

Heart-healthy oils, along with soy, flaxseed, and fish oils, are the best places to find large quantities of omega-3. Interestingly enough, men in countries where high amounts of fish are consumed demonstrate a lower risk of developing prostate cancer.

Can CoQ10 prevent or cure prostate cancer?

Coenzyme Q is known by many names, but most frequently it's called CoQ10. Almost every cell in the human body combines B vitamins, vitamin C, and amino acids to make CoQ10.

People who eat a well-balanced diet tend to have enough naturally occurring CoQ10. Whether supplemental CoQ10 could help in cardiovascular disease is unknown, but the studies so far have been disappointing. When tested for its effect on congestive heart failure, CoQ10 didn't work any better than a sugar pill. Another concern is that for men who are on blood-thinning drugs, taking CoQ10 can offset the effectiveness of those drugs.

Studies to date show only two groups of men who may benefit from taking CoQ10. The first group is men who are on high doses of cholesterol-lowering drugs. The body makes CoQ10 in part from a backbone of cholesterol. That's why some physicians suggest that their patients who are on cholesterol-lowering drugs also take CoQ10 supplements. (If you're on cholesterol medication, talk with your own doctor if you're thinking about taking CoQ10.)

The second group who may benefit from supplemental CoQ10 are those diagnosed with Parkinson's disease. A recent study showed that patients already diagnosed with Parkinson's disease may have lower levels of CoQ10 in their cells. Bear in mind this finding was for people who were already diagnosed with Parkinson's disease, not those who were merely concerned about having it.

There's been only one laboratory study of CoQ10 and prostate cancer, and CoQ10 didn't do anything in terms of hampering the growth of cancer cells.

Are there any herbal remedies or drugs used to treat enlarged prostates that also affect prostate cancer?

Some people mistakenly assume that because saw palmetto (see Chapter 1) helps alleviate benign prostatic hyperplasia (BPH), it can affect prostate cancer. But there's no proof to support this idea because no studies to date have been done on saw palmetto and cancer.

Finasteride and dutasteride are prescribed to treat BPH, and finasteride has been demonstrated in the Prostate Cancer Prevention Trial to reduce the risk of prostate cancer. Also, dutasteride has shown in some preliminary results that it may prevent prostate cancer; the drug is going to be tested in a large clinical trial. Results should be available in the next couple of years.

Do plant estrogen supplements provide benefit to prostate cancer patients?

In 2002, the Food and Drug Administration (FDA) removed one of these plant estrogen supplements, PC-SPES, from the market. But PC-SPES was only one of the several over-the-counter estrogenic (female hormone) supplements readily available.

Be aware that these supplements are similar to an estrogenic drug and can have serious effects. In general, these supplements decrease testosterone. Men who use these over-the-counter pills tend to experience a drop in prostate specific antigen (PSA) levels most likely because of the large drop in testosterone. In studies examining these herbal plant estrogens, men have reported side effects similar to hormonal or estrogen therapy—including erectile dysfunction, breast tenderness, and loss of body hair. In addition, these herbal estrogenic supplements could cause blood clots to form in the veins of the legs, which in some cases *can be fatal.*

Can aspirin prevent prostate cancer?

Studies show that men who take aspirin regularly to reduce their chance of heart attack also have a lower risk for prostate cancer. And when prostate cancer is diagnosed in the men who are on aspirin therapy, their risk of an aggressive cancer appears to be less.

In fact, being on aspirin therapy *may* be one of the smartest ways to help prevent prostate cancer. However, if something provides a medical benefit, it also comes with a catch. The daily use of aspirin is associated with an increased risk of internal bleeding or ulcers. So, before men try to put themselves on aspirin therapy for prostate cancer, they *must* discuss personal risk factors with their doctors. In younger men, the risk may be greater than the benefit because long-term exposure could lead to side effects.

One last fact about aspirin. Aspirin comes from willow bark, whose active ingredient is salicylic acid. Want to know where else salicylic acid is found? In most fruits and vegetables.

Lifestyle and Diet Following Diagnosis

Is there anything I can do to slow the growth of early stage prostate cancer?

There are several things that you can do to help yourself. Reducing the amount of saturated fat in your diet appears to be one of the best ways to impact prostate cancer. Substantially cutting down on saturated fat—dairy fat, the fat in red meats, and other animal fats—could slow the growth of the prostate cancer tumor. In a recent study in Quebec City, Canada, researchers carefully reviewed the diets of more than 425 prostate cancer patients. Their conclusion was that the number one factor from these patients' diets that favorably influenced prognosis was reducing saturated fat intake.[2]

No one is exactly sure why reducing saturated fat is beneficial in fighting cancer, but it could be that the structure of saturated fat "feeds" tumor growth. We recommend that saturated fat make up less than 10 percent of your daily calorie intake. Please note that it doesn't do any good to cut out excess amounts of saturated fat only to replace all of those calories with sugar. Prostate cancer seems to like a high caloric intake. In obese men, we're now seeing higher rates of prostate cancer. Obesity is also a problem because it not only increases the risk of being diagnosed with prostate cancer in the first place, but it can worsen the prognosis.

All of those extra calories in your diet can be sneaky. It is no secret that fast foods are typically high in calories. Did you know that when you "super-size" your fast-food meal, that 500-calorie meal jumps up to almost 1,500 calories? That's nearly an entire day's recommended intake!

Calories inch into our diets in other places, too. Twenty years ago, the average size soft drink was eight ounces and contained about 100 calories. Today the average size soft drink is 20 to 23 ounces and contains close to 300 calories. So, a little attention goes a long way in cutting out unnecessary calories.

What's the role of physical activity in prostate health?

There's some disagreement about whether physical activity reduces the risk of prostate cancer, but there are definitely some favorable studies indicating exercise helps overall prostate health. The best part about exercise is that there is little downside. Physical activity benefits mental and overall physical health. For those reasons alone, it makes sense for prostate cancer patients to incorporate more activity into their lives. It doesn't matter what you do—walking, swimming, jogging, rowing, or other activities. Just move your body regularly, and exercise enough to maintain a healthy body weight. In some individuals this means 30 minutes per day about three times a week, but in others it could mean 30 minutes per day seven days a week.

What role does soy play in prostate health?

In the countries that have a low risk of prostate cancer, foods with a high source of naturally occurring plant estrogens—such as soy—are regularly incorporated into the diet.

We recommend making soy a regular part of your diet, giving it as much priority as increasing fruits and vegetables and decreasing saturated fat. Soy is one of the only foods approved by the FDA that is allowed to advertise that it lowers the risk of heart disease.

If you've tried tofu and don't like it, try another soy product. Tofu is only *one* kind of soy food. Today many soy foods are on the market that weren't available even a couple of years ago—soy milk, soy cheese, soy nuts, and soy ice cream, for instance. There are also textured vegetable protein and commercially made meatless patties that look and taste similar to hamburger. There's such a diverse group of products now that you can take the same approach you do with fruits and vegetables—pick the ones that work for you and stick with them. If you try something and don't like it, don't give up on soy. Try another product and then another. Soon, you'll find a whole range of soy products that you'll eat.

An inexpensive way to get soy into the diet is to buy soybeans. The bean is extremely high in plant estrogen and soy protein. For the family that is really cost-conscious, soy protein powder, which can be mixed into baked goods or beverages, can last months and costs only a few dollars.

If you're thinking about splashing a bit of extra soy sauce on rice and calling that a serving of soy, think again. Soy sauce contains *none* of the beneficial soy compounds.

Does consuming flaxseed inhibit prostate cancer?

Flaxseed is a good source of a type of plant estrogen called lignans. In fact, flaxseed is the most concentrated source of lignans. Researchers at Duke University had men with prostate cancer use several servings of flaxseed daily and reduce their daily fat intake before they had their prostates removed.[3] In *one* month, the average cholesterol level dropped by 27 points and the subjects' PSA levels also decreased. The researchers found enough changes in the cancer cells to suggest that a fat-restricted diet supplemented with flaxseed may affect the biology of prostate cancer. It's too early to make a definite claim, but researchers say such findings warrant more study into this dietary approach.

Should I take flaxseed supplements?

In contrast to plain flaxseed that costs a few dollars for a month's supply, supplements are generally expensive. Many believe that flaxseed oil or flaxseed pills are the way to go, but the cheapest source—the seed itself—is as smart as any supplement.

There are many ways to get flaxseed into your diet. Sprinkle a table-spoon of flaxseed meal on your morning cereal. It doesn't really matter if you grind the seeds yourself in a coffee grinder or buy already-ground flaxseed meal from a health-food store. You can also consume the seeds without grinding them, although most human studies have used the ground form. You may just want to wash down a tablespoon of whole seeds with juice or water. If you don't like the flaxseed meal on your cereal and dislike the idea of downing a tablespoon of seeds with water or juice, not to worry. Adding a bit of ground flaxseed to muffin batter or other baked goods is a great way to get flaxseed into your daily routine.

There is one minor drawback to know about. Flaxseed is quite high in fiber. If you take it at the same time that you take other medications, it reduces the absorption of those prescription medicines. So, be sure to take flaxseed, even flaxseed oil, at a different time than you take prescription pills. Also, moderation is a good rule. One or two servings a day of flaxseed are all you need. In addition, remember that most cancer and cardiovascular studies have focused on the flaxseed itself, not the oil or the pills.

Is flaxseed better than flaxseed oil?

The oil comes from the seed. Taking the oil means you're actually deal-ing with an inferior product that's more expensive. If you want to save money, get the flaxseed. It's not that we don't think the oil is beneficial. If you can't tolerate the seed itself and don't like grinding it up, then con-suming the flaxseed oil does make sense. Be aware that the oil contains more calories, which is something to keep in mind if you're watching calo-rie consumption.

Supplements for Special Circumstances

Supplements and Radiation Therapy

For patients on external beam radiation or seed implantation, we recom-mend avoiding all dietary supplements during the therapy and for several months afterward. One of the ways radiation works is to create free radicals that destroy prostate cancer cells. Because some high-dose antioxidant pills are designed to destroy free radicals, they might interfere with radiation therapy. Once the radiation is complete or the radioactive prostate seeds have spent their energy, then it's reasonable to resume these supplements. This should usually take three to six months (depending on the half-life of the seed implant being used; talk with your doctor). During this time, it's a good idea to focus more on lifestyle changes (regular exercise, weight loss or maintenance, and a good diet).

We are in no way implying that any or all dietary supplements have been proven to reduce the effectiveness of your radiation treatment. The problem is that this has not been studied, and, in the meantime, it's better to be safe than sorry. In other words, why should the doctor or you take the chance of reducing the effectiveness of a proven prostate cancer treatment for an alternative treatment that has not been studied with radiation treatment? This does not seem wise until research determines what is and is not safe with radiation therapy.

If supplements are to be avoided during radiotherapy, what can I do to alleviate hot flashes caused by the hormones?

Some men undergo hormonal therapy alone or combined with radiation therapy. If you are experiencing hot flashes as a side effect of hormonal therapy, it's reasonable to use soy and/or flaxseed. Prescription medications can relieve hot flashes, as well. Ask your doctor.

I heard that long-term hormone therapy could cause osteoporosis. What can be done about this?

Osteoporosis is bone loss or a weakening of the bones. While women are more prone to osteoporosis as they age, some men also experience it. Furthermore, when men are on hormonal therapy, they may show an accelerated loss of bone. That's why it's important for men who are on long-term hormonal therapy (more than four months) to talk with their doctors about taking vitamin D and calcium supplements to help promote bone growth. The precise dosage of calcium and vitamin D will vary, depending on bone loss experienced before, during, or after treatment. First, talk to your doctor about getting an osteoporosis screening test. After this is complete, talk

again with him or her about any possible supplements and/or drug treatments for osteoporosis prevention.

A couple of final facts about calcium and vitamin D. These supplements appear to decrease the risk of colon cancer in high-risk patients, help
prevent fractures, and aid in cardiovascular health. A cardiovascular trial
showed that women who took calcium supplements for a year increased
their good cholesterol by 7 percent. Interestingly, the countries that have
the lowest rates of cardiovascular disease and prostate cancer also have the
lowest rates of bone fracture.

What is it about tomato products and other vegetables that seems to be beneficial for the prostate?

While it's true that men with a higher consumption of tomato products
seem to have a lower risk for prostate cancer, it's also true that these men
tend to have a lot of other healthy habits. They eat less saturated fat, exercise more, and maintain healthier weights.

Don't be fooled into thinking that somehow the tomato product is
superior to all other fruits and vegetables in terms of prostate health. The
active ingredient in tomatoes is lycopene. Lycopene is incorporated into the
prostate and seems to have an impact on prostate cancer growth. But
lycopene is found in many different foods including pink grapefruit, guava,
watermelon, and papaya.

There are lycopene supplements, but scientific data on the pill has been
weak, at best. Our advice is to save your money on the lycopene pill and
instead eat more fruits and vegetables.

Interestingly enough, as scientists are doing more research on broccoli,
cauliflower, spinach, and the like, they're finding these and other vegetables provide a benefit to the prostate. For example, even the so-called
"allium vegetables," such as dietary garlic (not garlic pills), may provide a
benefit. So, no, it's not *just* tomatoes that help prostate health. Stick with a
diversity of fruits and vegetables. It will keep you interested in eating them,
and it will expose you to the largest number of natural anticancer compounds.

I've heard that drinking green tea kills prostate cancer cells. True or false?

Many natural compounds in teas resemble some of the drugs we use in
cancer. Green tea specifically contains several compounds that seem to

impact cancer cell growth in the test tube. We already know that in countries that have a high green tea intake, there appears to be less prostate cancer.

So, the short answer is that green tea does appear to be effective for prevention and avoiding recurrence of prostate cancer. But there is little data on whether it provides additional benefits during treatment of localized or advanced prostate cancer.

There is one thing to keep in mind about green tea. It is one of the highest sources of vitamin K, which the body needs to form blood clots. Many cardiovascular patients are on blood thinners that work by decreasing the amount of vitamin K in the body. Since large amounts of green tea increase vitamin K, it can therefore decrease the effectiveness of prescription blood thinners.

Is it just green tea that provides all the benefits, or do black and herbal teas hold any promise?

The other teas seem to look as good as green teas right now. Many of them contain compounds similar to those found in green tea. Some substances found in black or herbal teas but not in green tea appear to provide some cardiovascular benefits, as well.

Do I have to cut out sugar and coffee now that I've been diagnosed?

We recommend that prostate cancer patients maintain the pleasures of life, but at a moderate level. We have not said that fast food *once in a while* is bad. We've said an *excessive* amount of fast food is bad. Some articles in the popular press erroneously tell you to eliminate *all* fat, chocolate, sugar, and the like. But the reality is that for a man who consumes these things in moderation, there's little to be concerned about. So, drinking a couple of cups of coffee a day is certainly okay.

What about alcohol?

Alcohol in moderation seems to have a benefit in terms of heart disease. Alcohol contains several estrogen-type compounds, so we're finding that a moderate amount of alcohol seems to have either no impact or decreases the risk of prostate cancer.

If I had to choose, which is more important—diet or exercise?

There's an effect called the momentum effect. It means that if you incorporate one healthy lifestyle change, chances are that you're going to naturally move to a second, then to a third. For instance, if you become concerned about your saturated fat intake, soon you'll probably become conscious of your weight, then your level of physical activity, and so on. The momentum effect works in a positive direction—if you're willing to start with one change.

Similarly, a negative momentum effect occurs. In patients who smoke, we are not only concerned about them smoking, we are also worried about the fact that these patients tend to be less physically active, eat fewer fruits and vegetables, and consume more saturated fat. For patients like these, the momentum of the pendulum has swung in the opposite direction.

How can I take advantage of the momentum effect?

Make your goal to work on one simple change, and then start working on the second, third, fourth, and more. We have observed that the men who incorporate the greatest number of lifestyle changes—avoiding excess saturated fat and calories, eating more fruits and vegetables, exercising, and incorporating soy and flaxseed into their daily diets—seem to experience the fewest side effects from radiation and hormonal therapy during prostate cancer treatment.

If I had to make one single lifestyle change to aid prostate health, what would that be?

Not one, but two things. First, pay as much attention to the levels of your healthful cholesterol (HDL, high-density lipoproteins) and unhealthful cholesterol (LDL, low-density lipoproteins) as you pay to your PSA. Every man (or his spouse) knows his PSA number. We advise that you know your cholesterol levels, too. Monitoring cholesterol as closely as monitoring the PSA level is a great foundation that provides insight into heart health and overall health risks.

Second, maintain a healthy weight. There's no question that science is seeing a link between weight gain, heart disease, and diabetes. Now we're beginning to see a negative impact on prognosis for overweight men with prostate cancer. Maintaining a healthful weight sounds mundane, but it's one of the hardest things you will do in your life because it involves doing everything that's healthy.

If I could add one thing to my diet to help in the battle against prostate cancer, what is it?

Again, not one, but two things—soy and flaxseed. If you add those, you do yourself a world of good in terms of cardiovascular—and prostate—health.

Once you become sensitive to looking for soy products, you're going to become sensitive to eating more fruits and vegetables, lowering overall calorie intake, decreasing saturated fat, and incorporating more omega-3 fatty acids. Again, as with weight loss and maintenance, adding soy and flaxseed into your diet seems simple but it takes commitment. However, it will lead to a positive momentum that can make a difference in your overall health.

I have been hearing and reading a lot about these low-carbohydrate (high-protein and high-fat) diets. Are low-carbohydrate diets a safe and effective way to lose weight?

Low-carbohydrate diets are getting a lot of publicity these days. A good thing about these diets is that they allow you to consume fat, which can be a very effective way to suppress the appetite. Fat in food is one of the most effective appetite suppressors, so individuals become less hungry and they consume fewer overall calories. However, low-carbohydrate diets are also very restrictive. They do not allow you to eat a variety of healthy foods. So, the bad news about these diets is that they are not only too extreme (similar to a low-fat diet), but many researchers also question the long-term safety of these diets.

Our take is that with proper and regular exercise, most individuals do not need to adopt a low-carbohydrate diet. Plus, these diets are tough to stick with over several years. However, for the small number of individuals who have tried just about everything to reduce weight and are frustrated, low-carbohydrate diets may be a good "jump start" to weight loss. After several months, we suggest that you return to an "everything in moderation" approach, as outlined in this chapter, along with regular exercise to achieve the best overall results.

Keep in mind that 3,500 calories equal one pound. Therefore, if you were to just reduce your overall calories by 500 per day for seven days and not exercise at all, you would lose just one pound per week! This fact may help you understand that long-term weight loss takes a lot of time and com-mitment. It's not easy, but just by reducing calories and exercising it is pos-sible to lose a couple of pounds a week over a long period of time. Remember, patience and commitment are the keys to long-term weight loss.

Remember, too, that certain weight loss programs such as Weight Watchers and others may also be effective ways to lose weight. If you are frustrated about weight loss, do not try to solve this problem on your own. Ask your doctor about the latest advice, programs, and medications to achieve the weight loss you need.

3

How Do They Test for Prostate Cancer?

Deborah A. Kuban, M.D.; Ian M. Thompson, M.D.;
John C. Blasko, M.D.

DRE. PSA. CT. MRI. TNM. ng/mL. Sounds a bit like alphabet soup, doesn't it? Those are really just some of the important shorthands the medical profession uses when talking about screening, diagnosing, and staging prostate cancer.

We devote this chapter to explaining the broad categories of tests patients may encounter before treatment: screening exams, tissue analysis, and imaging procedures, as well as how doctors grade and stage prostate cancer.

Although we touch upon most of the tests in the world of prostate cancer, the type and number of tests each individual patient will undergo depends upon how advanced his cancer is and the chosen treatment. If you opt for surgery you will get a different set of tests than another patient who selects watchful waiting. While we provide a broad picture of screening and diagnostic procedures, if you have any questions about any test or results, talk with your own physician. He or she is absolutely your best advocate throughout this stage of your journey.

Screening Tests

When should I be tested for prostate cancer?

There is no "correct" age to begin screening for prostate cancer. The risk of developing prostate cancer before age 50 is low. That's why many experts recommend the average man whose life expectancy is at least 10 years beyond age 50 start getting his annual prostate cancer tests at 50. Men at higher risk—African-American men and any man who has a strong family history of the disease (father, brother, or son diagnosed with prostate cancer)—should begin testing at age 45. Some men who are especially anxious about prostate cancer might talk with their doctors about whether they would benefit from starting their annual tests at an even younger age.

What tests are used to screen for prostate cancer?

Screening tests are those that people undergo to find out who does and does not have a particular disease or condition. The digital rectal exam (DRE) and the prostate specific antigen (PSA) blood test are the two standard screening tests for prostate cancer detection.

During a DRE, the physician inserts a gloved finger inside the rectum to examine the part of the prostate that's closest to the rectal wall. The physician is searching for any areas that feel abnormal, or have an unusual firmness or a lump (nodule). Such an abnormality *may* indicate the presence of prostate cancer. Simply because the doctor feels an irregularity doesn't mean it's prostate cancer.

In most prostate cancer cases diagnosed today, the DRE does not reveal a nodule the doctor can feel (palpate). This is either because the cancer is small and well-hidden within the normal tissue or it's located in a portion of the gland that's inaccessible from the rectal area. It's the PSA blood test that usually finds these early, nonpalpable tumors.

What's the PSA blood test?

Prostate specific antigen is an enzyme produced by the prostate. Recall from Chapter 1 that semen coagulates after ejaculation, and the PSA enzyme helps turn the congealed semen back into liquid so sperm can swim freely and fertilization may take place. It's normal for small amounts of PSA to "leak" into a man's bloodstream. The PSA blood test measures nanograms (one thousand-millionth of a gram) of PSA per milliliter of serum (the liquid part of blood), and it's written as ng/mL.

Noncancerous conditions, such as benign prostatic hyperplasia (BPH), prostate inflammation, prostate infection, or trauma, can elevate PSA because these conditions may cause more of the enzyme to seep into the bloodstream. An elevated PSA does not necessarily indicate cancer. It only points to something that needs further investigation.

Although a large number of men undergo annual screening, PSA testing has never been scientifically proven to reduce the risk of dying from prostate cancer. Because false positives can lead to unnecessary biopsies— and a biopsy is an invasive procedure—not everyone in the medical establishment universally recommends this screening procedure.

The National Cancer Institute started the multi-institutional Prostate, Lung, Colorectal, Ovarian (PLCO) cancer screening trial in 1993 to explore whether screening for a number of cancers, including prostate, is valuable. Early findings of the PLCO trial suggest that if the PSA level is less than 1.0 ng/mL, then the patient could reduce testing to once every five years. If this PSA test is lower than 2.0 ng/mL, then the doctor might suggest getting the PSA re-tested every other year. And anyone with a PSA level above 2.0 ng/mL should continue to get a yearly PSA test. Your own doctor, however, will make screening recommendations based on your personal medical history.

What is a normal PSA reading?

The upper limit of a "normal" PSA initially was thought to be 4.0 ng/mL. This level comes from screening studies that contained groups of men of various ages. The goal was to choose a PSA level that would be as sensitive as possible to cancer but not so low that many men with minimally increased PSA from benign causes would be unnecessarily biopsied. The most recent information has suggested that it may be reasonable to consider lowering the *normal* PSA level to 2.5 or 3.0 ng/mL, particularly for younger men. The reason for this is that while the likelihood of a positive biopsy in the 4.0–10.0 ng/mL range is about 25 percent, the likelihood of a positive biopsy in the 2.5–4.0 ng/mL range drops only a bit, to 15 percent to 20 percent. For some men, this one-in-five risk may be sufficiently high to consider a biopsy if their PSA falls in this range.

What is age-adjusted PSA?

Prostate specific antigen levels tend to increase as a man ages and his prostate volume increases. What may be a normal amount of PSA for a man at age 50 will be different by the time he reaches 70. For instance, if a man is younger than 50 and has a PSA of 4.5 ng/mL, his doctor might call for a biopsy. But if a 75-year-old's PSA is 4.5 ng/mL, his doctor might consider this normal for his age and not request additional tests. (See Table 3.1.)

Be aware that age-adjusted PSA levels are controversial and not everyone in the medical community agrees about their accuracy or usefulness. It has been suggested that while age-adjusted PSA levels may pick up more cancers in the younger age group by using lower "normal" PSA levels, more cancer may be missed in older patients.

What is free PSA?

Most PSA binds to other proteins in the blood. Because this PSA is "complexed" or bonded to these proteins, it's often called "complexed PSA." The remaining unattached PSA is termed "free PSA." Because the type of PSA varies with different kinds of prostate tissue, men with a *lower* percentage of free PSA have a higher risk for prostate cancer. For example, a man whose total PSA is 8.0 ng/mL with 8 percent free PSA has a greater chance of having prostate cancer than his next-door neighbor whose total PSA also is 8.0 ng/mL but with 35 percent free PSA.

TABLE 3.1   Age-Adjusted Prostate Specific Antigen

This table of age-adjusted PSA, unlike others, maximizes sensitivity, which means these levels are least likely to miss a prostate cancer.

Age Range	Worrisome PSA Level
40 – 50	> 2.5 ng/mL
50 – 60	> 3.0 ng/mL
60 – 70	> 3.5 ng/mL
70 +	> 4.0 ng/mL

A free PSA test may be requested if the PSA is between 4.0 and 10.0 ng/mL. If the test shows a low level of free PSA (usually less than 15 percent to 20 percent), biopsy is often the next step. If that biopsy turns out negative, it's common for the doctor to ask the patient to come back for another biopsy in six months or a year. This is because a low level of free PSA means something may be going on that bears watching.

However, a man who is found to have a high percentage of free PSA is not guaranteed to be without prostate cancer. In some cases, a biopsy of a nodule may turn up prostate cancer despite a low overall total PSA *and* a high level of free PSA.

What is PSA density and is it useful in determining if I have prostate cancer?

Larger prostates tend to produce more PSA simply because there's more glandular tissue to create that enzyme. This means that more PSA is available to escape into the blood. If the patient has a large prostate, an elevated PSA level may arouse less suspicion of prostate cancer. The problem with this reasoning is that a cancer can easily be overlooked in men with larger prostates.

In short, most studies have shown that the PSA itself is more predictive of prostate cancer than PSA density. For this reason, PSA density is not used in deciding whether to do a biopsy.

What is PSA density of the transition zone?

Prostate specific antigen density of the transition zone is a mathematical calculation. Two pieces of information are needed to arrive at this number. First is the PSA level, expressed in ng/mL. Second is the size of the central portion of prostate measured in cubic centimeters; this measurement is achieved by using an ultrasound probe. The PSA value is divided by the measured volume. While some academic institutions have suggested that an upper limit of 0.15 correlates to a higher incidence of cancer and may signal the need for biopsy, very few institutions in the United States use it because it is a complex and expensive test.

What is PSA velocity?

Prostate specific antigen velocity is the rate at which PSA rises over time. If the PSA rises less than 0.75 ng/mL in a given year, we usually don't worry.

A PSA level that rises faster than that hints at something unusual. If your PSA has climbed more than 0.75 ng/mL in less than a year regardless of the absolute level of PSA, your physician may call for further testing.

Does ejaculation increase the PSA level?

Yes, ejaculation can increase the PSA level in the some men. The increase, however, is usually minimal and the PSA usually returns to normal within 48 hours. If a man wants to minimize the risk of his PSA being elevated, he should avoid ejaculation for a few days before the PSA test.

How do I know if a prostate infection has elevated my PSA?

Infection of the prostate can cause inflammation and elevate the PSA level. The usual symptoms of a prostate infection are increased urinary frequency and discomfort in the pelvis. Prostate infections are sometimes hard to diagnose. While a urinalysis is the best test to evaluate an infection of the bladder, it may not detect infection of the prostate. In other words, a negative urinalysis does not mean the prostate is not infected. A second step is often a massage of the prostate to express fluid, which is then examined microscopically for signs of infection. If the physician still suspects an infection in the prostate, an antibiotic may be prescribed. The medication will kill the offending bacteria, and the PSA level should decrease in several weeks to months. If the PSA does not decrease, a biopsy may be recommended.

How many PSA tests should be done to determine the need for biopsy? How much time should I wait between these tests?

It is important to find out if something other than cancer is causing the PSA increase. If infection or inflammation is not causing the PSA rise, a biopsy is the usual next step. If this biopsy is negative and the PSA remains elevated, a repeat biopsy may be recommended, often taking a larger number of biopsy samples. If the repeat biopsy is again negative, the patient will usually undergo repeat PSA tests at 6- to 12-month intervals. The physician may recommend subsequent biopsies based on changes in PSA, changes in the DRE, or the doctor's level of concern.

What other blood tests might be used?

An older test, prostatic acid phosphatase (PAP), measures another enzyme produced by the prostate. Although some men with prostate cancer have increased amounts of prostatic acid phosphatase, this test is not nearly as good at picking up early prostate cancer as the PSA test. That's why PAP is rarely used anymore as a screening method.

It is true that a high PAP level can signal locally advanced or metastatic disease in men who have already been diagnosed with prostate cancer. But other factors, such as a PSA level and the Gleason score (explained later), are generally better predictors of the cancer's extent than PAP.

Can I have prostate cancer and not show **any** *symptoms or an elevated PSA?*

The vast majority of patients with early stage prostate cancer don't have symptoms, which is why getting both regular PSA tests and DREs is important. If the PSA level and the DRE are both normal, there's little need for additional testing because the chance of a positive biopsy under these conditions is very low.

That being said, however, up to 25 percent of prostate cancers do not cause a PSA elevation. These may be high-grade (meaning faster-growing) tumors that have lost the ability to produce PSA like their normal prostate cell counterparts. That's why there's no increase in PSA. A nodule or firmness may be the only way to detect these types of tumors. This is just one more example of why DREs and PSA tests are used together.

Tissue Tests

How is a prostate biopsy performed?

A biopsy simply means removing and microscopically examining several pieces of tissue from the prostate. Most physicians use an ultrasound-guided technique for prostate biopsies, which involves inserting an ultrasound probe into the rectum to view the prostate. This may be slightly uncomfortable but it's usually not painful.

Using a guide that's attached to the probe, the doctor directs the needle to a specific area and then triggers the rapid, automated biopsy unit. The needle removes a very small core of tissue in a split second. Separate needle sticks remove 6 to 12 samples (called core biopsies) in rapid succession. Many physicians today use local anesthesia around the prostate to minimize pain from a biopsy.

The entire biopsy process lasts only a few minutes and most men experience few side effects. Common minor side effects are a small amount of bleeding from the rectum or urine and blood in the semen. It's important to recognize that small amounts of blood in the semen can persist for several weeks.

To reduce the risk of bleeding, we usually tell patients to avoid aspirin, anticoagulants such as Coumadin, and nonsteroidal anti-inflammatory medications such as ibuprofen for a week prior to the biopsy. We might also prescribe antibiotics to reduce the chance of infection following the biopsy.

What is an adequate number of cores to take for a prostate biopsy— six, 10, or 12?

There is no "best" number of biopsy cores, but initial studies a number of years ago considered sextant biopsies (six cores) standard. Sextant biopsies remove samples from the base, mid-gland, and apex on both left and right lobes of the prostate (see Figure 3.1).

Many studies now show that increasing the number of cores from six to 10 or 12 will identify more men with significant prostate cancer. These additional samples usually come from the outside edges of the gland (see Figure 3.2). If we suspect the cancer is in the front (anterior) or central part of the gland, one or two samples may be taken from this area, too.

Taking these additional cores has the advantage of reducing the risk of missing important cancer. Plus, these additional cores may reduce the need for a repeat biopsy if this first biopsy turns out to be negative.

Will the biopsy find prostate cancer on the first try?

In about 75 percent of men with an elevated PSA, the biopsy will be negative. For some of these men, however, a number of circumstances may lead to the recommendation of a repeat biopsy. The risk factors may include (1) a worrisome DRE, (2) a clearly elevated PSA, (3) a rising PSA, (4) a strong family history of prostate cancer, and (5) precancerous changes found in the first biopsy. When the biopsy should be repeated is a matter of some debate. Certainly the greater the concern about prostate cancer risk, the sooner the repeat biopsy can be done. This is where the advice and counsel of your own physician is important.

FIGURE 3.1   Sextant Biopsy

The general locations of the six cores when a sextant prostate biopsy is performed.

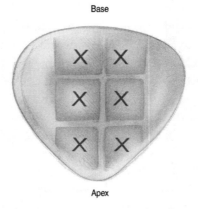

FIGURE 3.2   Ten-Core Biopsy

This figure represents the areas where samples are taken when a 10-core prostate biopsy is done.

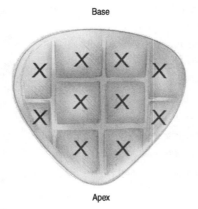

What's the pathologist looking for in the cores?

Prostate cancer has particular, well-known features that distinguish it from the normal prostate cells that form small glands within the prostate. The pathologist is looking for changes in the shape and size of these cells and glands.

The pathologist will examine the pattern of the cancer cells and assign a number from one to five to the most common pattern seen. A grade of 1 denotes cancerous cells that are most like normal cells (these cells are known as well-differentiated cells), and a grade of 5 is assigned to cells that are the most malignant (these cells are poorly differentiated cells; see Figure 3.3).

The pathologist then identifies the second most common pattern and again assigns a grade of 1 to 5. The two grades are added together to create the Gleason score. All Gleason scores range from 2 to 10. Most prostate cancers diagnosed today have Gleason scores of 5, 6, or 7. The more aggressive prostate cancers are 8, 9, and 10. Gleason grade 2, 3, or 4 prostate cancer is uncommon these days and almost never seen on a needle biopsy.

FIGURE 3.3   Gleason Grades

To arrive at the Gleason score, a pathologist will look at the types of cells in a biopsy core. Cancerous cells that are more similar to normal cells are called well-differentiated cells. Well-differentiated cells have a grade of 1. As the cells become less differentiated, their numeric grade increases. A grade of 5 is assigned to those cells that are the most malignant and poorly differentiated. The pathologist identifies the two patterns of cancer cells that occur most frequently in the sample and assigns a grade to each. The two numbers are then added to arrive at a Gleason score.

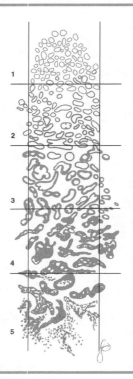

Lower Gleason scores indicate more slow-growing tumors that are more likely to be contained within the prostate gland (localized) for a longer time. These tumors may not even require treatment in older men. Higher Gleason scores behave just the opposite. They tend to spread rapidly and aggressive treatment is often recommended.

What's on the pathology report?

A pathology report includes crucial information such as the number of cores and where they were taken (the right base, for instance); the type of cancer (such as adenocarcinoma); the Gleason grade and score (grade 3 + grade 4 = Gleason score 7); if there's evidence of perineural invasion; and how much cancer was found in each core (5 percent, for example). All of this can help to predict the chance that the cancer is still contained in the prostate.

What does perineural invasion mean?

Nerve branches originate in the pelvis and some of those branches enter the prostate capsule, while others course along the outside of the gland and down to the penis (see Figure 3.4). Those nerves that penetrate the prostate may provide a means for the cancer cells to escape and travel beyond the prostate. *Peri-* is a prefix that means "near, around, or enclosing." So, *perineural invasion* means the pathologist has detected cancer spreading along nerves within the prostate.

The medical community disagrees on whether perineural invasion on a biopsy report can be relied on to predict whether the cancer has escaped the prostate. In 38 to 50 percent of needle biopsies in which a pathologist reports perineural invasion, at the time of surgery cancer is found to have spread beyond the capsule. However, when entire prostates with prostate cancer are examined following surgical removal, almost all of them have some perineural invasion. That's why the finding of perineural invasion carries less weight in predicting the extent of the disease than stage, grade, and PSA.

What does "PIN" mean on a pathology report?

The acronym PIN stands for *p*rostatic *i*ntraepithelial *n*eoplasia. *Intraepithelial* means "within the epithelium"—the cells that line the glandular ducts of the prostate. In this case, the normal cells that line the prostate ducts have been replaced by cells that have many features of a cancer cell; while these individual cells *look* like cancer cells, PIN is *not* cancer because these cells have not invaded the prostate.

FIGURE 3.4   Nerves Near the Prostate

Nerves that penetrate the prostate may be how cancer cells escape and travel outside of the gland.

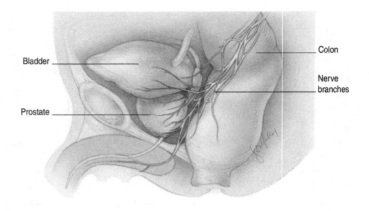

Some pathologists think that PIN may be a precursor of prostate cancer. The evidence suggesting that PIN may be the forerunner of cancer includes the fact that the PIN cells have a number of cancer features, as mentioned above, and PIN is commonly found adjacent to areas of cancer.

What does "atypia" mean on a biopsy report?

Atypia is the scientific shorthand for "atypical hyperplasia." Hyperplasia is an overgrowth of normal cells. Atypical hyperplasia is an overgrowth of cells that are somewhat abnormal but do not have the characteristics of cancer. The implications of "atypia" are not well understood and are a matter of some debate. It is not clear at this time if atypia predisposes an individual to a higher risk of cancer.

If the biopsy shows atypia or PIN, should the biopsy be repeated?

If the pathologist finds atypia, most physicians currently do not recommend another biopsy but may recommend a second pathologist review the sample, just to be sure.

When it comes to PIN, the answer is usually the opposite. In many men with PIN, a repeat biopsy has a 30 percent to 60 percent chance of finding cancer, which is why most physicians will recommend another biopsy. How long to wait before repeating the biopsy is really up to you and your doctor. While waiting a month or two can allow the inflammation from the first biopsy to subside, a pathologist would have no problem interpreting biopsy results if the patient went ahead with another biopsy right away. Many patients prefer a second biopsy quickly to reduce the anxiety of "not knowing."

What is a pelvic lymph node dissection?

A pelvic lymph node dissection is the surgical removal of some groups of lymph nodes in the pelvis to find out if the prostate cancer has spread. Lymph node dissection is most often done during a radical prostatectomy (total surgical removal of the prostate). In some instances, though, some pelvic lymph nodes are removed for examination even if the patient does not have a prostatectomy. This is done by a means of a laparoscope—a slender tube inserted into the abdomen through a tiny incision—or a separate open operation.

How can I determine if my urologist has sent the biopsy to a reputable lab for examination?

Laboratories are accredited and individual pathologists are credentialed. An accurate biopsy reading is very important because it helps guide the physician's treatment decisions.

Before sending cores for testing, the physician should be familiar with the expertise of the lab and the pathologist. Major cancer centers or universities that are recognized for prostate cancer treatment have pathologists on staff who are highly experienced in diagnosing and grading prostate cancer.

If you have *any* questions pertaining to the results, talk to your physician about your concerns and find out what your doctor thinks about sending the cores to an expert prostate pathologist for evaluation. Note, too, that if your insurance does not pay for a second reading, you may end up paying for it yourself.

What circumstances would suggest to my urologist or a pathologist that a second opinion is needed on the biopsy specimen?

Four general conditions would prompt a physician to seek a second opinion on a biopsy specimen:

1. If the pathologist is uncertain as to whether cancer is present
2. If there is a very tiny amount of early, low-grade cancer or suspicious cells
3. If the initial pathologist is not experienced in diagnosing and grading prostate cancer, or the report fails to state all of the important features of the cancer (such as biopsy site, Gleason pattern score, and amount of cancer in each needle biopsy sample)
4. If low-grade cancer is diagnosed on a needle biopsy (Gleason score 2, 3, or 4, but such scores are virtually always seen only on transurethral resection of the prostate [TURP] biopsies, not needle biopsies)

Can biopsy errors occur?

A biopsy error is extremely rare because each lab has quality assurance procedures in place to help keep this from happening. Pathologists are *very* careful to be sure that cancer is or is not present before they report their findings. If there is any question regarding the diagnosis, they can ask for a second opinion. Many pathologists take the extra step of having their colleagues confirm the diagnosis before issuing a report. However, a prostate cancer diagnosis can be a difficult determination and even the most experienced of prostate cancer pathologists can disagree on the diagnosis from time to time.

What is ploidy analysis and what can it show?

Ploidy analysis examines the DNA content of cells. The general rule is that the more malignant a cell is, the greater the amount of DNA in the cell's nucleus. This is because cancer is an uncontrolled growth of cells and the DNA is the first to replicate as the abnormal cell gets ready to divide. Because ploidy analysis can gauge an abnormal amount of DNA, it seems to be a measure of the degree of malignancy. The ploidy reading can vary from one place to another in an individual's cancer. Most experienced physicians feel that ploidy analysis is of much less value than the grade, stage, PSA, and the number of positive biopsy cores in calculating a tumor's aggressiveness. Since ploidy analysis usually does not add any information that would help us in recommending treatment options, we don't order this test.

Imaging Tests

What is a CT scan and what can it tell my doctor about whether or not I have prostate cancer?

A CT scan (also called a CAT scan) uses a computer to combine x-ray images to create cross-sectional or three-dimensional images of an organ. CT scans cannot reliably *detect* prostate cancer. Nor can they reliably predict if it has spread outside the gland. Unless the prostate cancer is quite large, a CT scan may not be able to see the tumor at all. CT scans can show enlarged pelvic lymph nodes, but they can't predict if those lymph nodes are cancerous. This is why a biopsy or surgical removal is the most reliable way to assess if the cancer has migrated to the pelvic lymph nodes.

What is the endorectal MRI?

An endorectal MRI is another imaging method to determine whether the cancer has spread outside the prostate capsule and/or into nearby structures. It's similar to a CT scan except instead of using x-rays, the imaging is done using a strong magnetic field. A small probe in the rectum (endorectal) allows the MRI to create detailed images of the prostate anatomy, urethra, and the neurovascular bundles.

While initial studies suggested that endorectal MRI might be helpful, most subsequent evaluations have found it not particularly useful in determining if cancer has spread outside the prostate. This is not surprising because when spread occurs it is so small that it is often detectable only with a microscope.

With PSA under 15–20 ng/mL, there is a low risk of the cancer in the lymph nodes. Imaging scans in these circumstances is almost always unfruitful and can sometimes mistakenly suggest spread of the disease when the cancer is actually confined to the gland.

To summarize, neither a CT scan nor an MRI offers much additional help in determining spread of the cancer. Both CT and MRI can detect enlargement of pelvic lymph nodes that may be related to cancer spread.

However, benign factors such as a biopsy or infection can lead to lymph node enlargement.

What is MRS?

Magnetic resonance spectroscopy (MRS; also called MRSI) is a relatively new technology. As with MRI, it uses a strong magnetic field and radio waves. Along with creating detailed pictures of the anatomy, MRS noninvasively gathers information about certain cellular chemicals, the concentrations of which are different in cancerous and normal cells. Abnormal amounts of these chemicals can indicate places where the cancer is present.

Early studies have suggested that combining MRI and MRS may not only help determine the aggressiveness of cancerous tumors contained within the prostate, but may also aid in assessing if and how far cancer has spread inside and possibly outside of the gland. Knowing if the cancer has spread, even in microscopic amounts, is vital in picking the best therapy. But currently MRI/MRS is not used routinely because more studies are needed to validate its effectiveness.

Can ultrasound detect prostate cancer?

Ultrasound helps in guiding the needle into the proper position within the prostate at the time of biopsy. But ultrasound, by itself, cannot reliably detect prostate cancer and is rarely helpful in determining the cancer's stage. While many have tried to correlate ultrasound findings with the presence of cancer, it's now apparent that the ultrasound images don't do a good job of accurately identifying prostate cancer. Cancer, especially in its earliest stages, may not be seen on ultrasound. Likewise, areas that appear abnormal are not always cancerous. Biopsy is always required to make a definitive diagnosis.

What do hypoechoic and hyperechoic refer to in an ultrasound report?

The rectal ultrasound probe emits sound waves that travel into the prostate. The sounds bounce back (echo) to create an image. The more solid or irregular the tissue, the more dense it is. This density allows the sound waves to bounce back to the ultrasound probe. This creates an image on the screen that is hyper (*hyper* means "more") echoic. These areas appear white on the screen. If the tissue is less dense, the image appears black because there is less tissue to reflect the sound waves. For instance, if there's calcium in the prostate we would see an intensely white image because the calcium reflects much of the sound waves. On the other hand, cystic (water-filled) and low-density areas allow sound waves to travel through without reflection. Since no echoes come back, these areas would appear black on the screen.

A prostate with mixed changes may have some regions that are more hypoechoic (black) and some that are more hyperechoic (white). During the early years of prostate ultrasound, it was thought the cancer was generally hypoechoic. Subsequently, it has been demonstrated that cancer can have almost *any* ultrasound pattern. It is for this reason that ultrasound is not used for cancer detection and screening.

What is color Doppler ultrasound?

Tumors often create blood vessels around them as they grow. Color Doppler ultrasound uses a special type of analysis to find areas of increased blood vessels within the prostate. While it would seem to make sense that the areas with more blood vessels might harbor regions of prostate cancer, most studies have found color Doppler ultrasound to be unreliable in finding cancer or determining its extent.

What is a bone scan and when is it needed?

In its later stages, prostate cancer tends to spread to bone. The cancer's activity in bone causes some bone to be reabsorbed while new bone is being created. The best way to detect this action, called bone remodeling, is with a bone scan. Fortunately, most men diagnosed with prostate cancer today do not have spread of cancer to the bone. In fact, if the PSA is less than 20 ng/mL and if the Gleason score is 7 or less, the risk of detectable spread to the bone is less than 1 percent. That's why a bone scan is rarely recommended under these circumstances.

How is a bone scan performed?

Bone scans are usually conducted in a hospital's nuclear medicine department. A small amount of radioactive material, called a radionuclide, is injected into the bloodstream through a vein in the arm. (The radionuclide is not dangerous, and the body rids itself of this substance through the urine within 24 hours.)

It takes a couple of hours for the radioactive substance to circulate throughout the body after it's injected; the scan itself takes only about an hour. The patient lies down and a flat disc (the gamma camera) is positioned over the patient to record the sites where the radionuclide accumulates. More of the radionuclide settles in the areas where bone is changing or growing rapidly.

Cancer is not the only reason the radionuclide collects in bone. Arthritis, injuries, old fractures, and even dental work show up during bone scans.

What happens if the bone scan shows suspicious areas?
If the gamma camera detects an abnormality, the usual next step is an x-ray, CT, or MRI to better evaluate that particular area.

I've heard some talk about a ProstaScint scan. What is it, and is it valuable in detecting the spread of prostate cancer?
A ProstaScint scan images molecules relatively specific to prostate cells. In a ProstaScint scan, another substance is mixed with the radionuclide before injection. This mixture attaches itself to prostate membrane specific antigen (PSMA), large concentrations of which can indicate either prostate cells or prostate cancer. While on occasion the test can locate groups of cancer cells outside the prostate, it is unreliable, often suggesting cancer spread when none has occurred. It is for this reason that few prostate cancer specialists rely on the ProstaScint scan.

Classification Systems
I've heard about stages and grades of prostate cancer. What does each term mean and why are they important?

- **Stage.** Stage is the determination of the extent of the cancer—whether it's confined to the prostate, if it has spread to nearby tissues, or if it has metastasized (spread by way of the lymphatic system or blood vessels) to other parts of the body. Unfortunately, it is never possible to predict or detect the spread with 100 percent accuracy.

    There are two types of staging you should be aware of—*clinical staging* and *pathologic staging*. Clinical staging is based on the information the doctor acquires before treatment begins. The DRE is the primary means of clinical staging. Additional tests, such as a bone scan or lymph node dissection, can influence the staging. The doctor's determination of clinical stage is essential in recommending a treatment. (Note that PSA and Gleason scoring are important in terms of prognosis and treatment selection but are *not* a part of staging.)

Pathologic staging refers to a pathologist's examination of the lymph nodes and prostate gland after removal. This staging can provide more exact information about tumor extension outside of the prostate, into the seminal vesicles, or to the lymph nodes and can help in determining prognosis.

- **Grade.** *Grade* is not the same as *stage*. The pathologist grades the prostate cancer from Gleason score 2 to 10 based on how aggressive it looks under the microscope. More aggressive cancers have a different appearance under the microscope than less aggressive malignancies.

How do I make sense of cancer staging?

After all of the tests are done, the medical team carefully reviews the information it has gathered about a particular patient's cancer to assign it a "stage." Staging gives medical practitioners a common language to discuss the patient's current condition, treatment, and prognosis. The most commonly used classification system is TNM (*T* stands for "tumor," *N* means "lymph nodes," and *M* designates "metastasis"). Since the TNM system was first developed, it has undergone frequent review to ensure that the classifications are as accurate as possible. Minor changes are made from time to time, and the American Joint Committee on Cancer (AJCC) regularly publishes its updates for physicians. You might run across slightly different TNM tables as you read other materials. Table 3.2 is based on the AJCC 2002 update.

What will the Gleason score tell me about my cancer?

The higher the Gleason score, the more aggressive the cancer is and the more likely it is to have spread outside the prostate. The Gleason score is used along with stage and PSA to determine the risk of spread outside the gland. Tumors with a Gleason 2 through 6 generally carry a low risk of spread. Gleason 7 has a moderate risk of spread. Gleason 8, 9, or 10 tumors have a moderately high likelihood of spread outside the gland.

What are low-, intermediate-, and high-risk groups?

Low-, intermediate-, and high-risk groups are merely a means to classify patients with similar probable outcomes (prognosis). This grouping is usually based on the three factors of stage, grade, and PSA. Patients can have different stages, Gleason scores, and PSAs, yet still have similar prognoses. There are some differing viewpoints about the cutoffs of certain measures

TABLE 3.2   AJCC Staging, Prostate

Primary Tumor		
	Clinical	**Pathologic (pT)**
TX	The tumor cannot be assessed	
T0	No evidence of a primary tumor	
T1	Clinically inapparent tumor neither palpable nor visible by imaging	
	T1a—Tumor incidental histologic finding in 5 percent or less of tissue resected	
	T1b—Tumor incidental histologic finding in more than 5 percent of tissue resected	
	T1c—Tumor identified by needle biopsy (e.g., because of elevated PSA)	
T2	Tumor confined within the prostate*	pT2*—Organ-confined
	T2a—Tumor involves one-half of one lobe or less	pT2a—Unilateral, involving one-half of one lobe or less
	T2b—Tumor involves more than one-half of one lobe but not both lobes	pT2b—Unilateral involving more than one-half of one lobe but not both lobes
	T2c—Tumor involves both lobes	pT2c—Bilateral disease
T3	Tumor extends through the prostate capsule**	pT3—Extraprostatic extension
	T3a—Extracapsular extension (unilateral or bilateral)	pT3a—Extraprostatic extension**
	T3b—Tumor invades seminal vesicle(s)	pT3b—Seminal vesicle invasion
T4	Tumor is fixed or invades adjacent structures other than seminal vesicles: bladder neck, external sphincter, rectum, levator muscles, and or/pelvic wall	pT4—Invasion of bladder, rectum

Note: Tumor found in one or both lobes by needle biopsy, but not palpable or reliably visible by imaging, is classified as T1c.

**Note: Invasion into the prostatic apex or into (but not beyond) the prostatic capsule is classified not as T3 but as T2.*

Note: There is no pathologic T1 classification.

**Note: Positive surgical margin should be indicated by an R1 descriptor (residual microscopic disease).*

TABLE 3.2   AJCC Staging, Prostate *(continued)*

Regional Lymph Nodes (N)		
	Clinical	**Pathologic**
NX	Regional lymph nodes were not assessed	pNX—Regional nodes not sampled
N0	No regional lymph node metastasis	pN0—No positive regional nodes
N1	Metastasis in regional lymph nodes(s)	pN1—Metastases in regional nodes

Distant Metastasis (M)*		
	Clinical	
MX	Distant metastasis cannot be assessed (not evaluated by any modality)	
M0	No distant metastasis	
M1	Distant metastasis	
	M1a—Nonregional lymph node(s)	
	M1b—Bone(s)	
	M1c—Other site(s) with or without bone disease	
	Note: When more than one site of metastasis is present, the most advanced category is used. pM1c is most advanced.	

Used with permission of the American Joint Committee on Cancer (AJCC), Chicago, Illinois. The original source for this material is the *AJCC Cancer Staging Manual, Sixth Edition* (2002) published by Springer-Verlag New York, www.springer-ny.com.

for the low-, intermediate-, and high-risk groups (see Table 3.3 for today's commonly used risk groupings in prostate cancer), but the important point to remember is that patients in the low-risk group have the greatest chance that their cancer will be cured. They also have a low risk of recurrence. Patients in the high-risk group have a lower chance their cancer will be cured and a higher risk of recurrence. Intermediate-risk patients are somewhere in between.

What do **early stage, locally advanced,** *and* **metastatic disease** *mean?*
Information about a tumor's stage influences the risk group into which a patient falls. The term *early stage* is applied to small- to medium-size tumors that have a better likelihood of being totally contained within the prostate.

Locally advanced cancer is thought of as a tumor that has spread outside the prostate capsule to the immediately surrounding area or to the seminal vesicles or bladder but not necessarily to the bones.

Metastatic disease means the cancer has spread to lymph nodes or other sites such as bone, lung, and liver, and it's treated differently than localized disease.

What are Partin Tables?

These tables, arranged by tumor stage, Gleason score, and initial PSA level, predict the chance of the cancer being outside the prostate capsule, in the seminal vesicles, or in the lymph nodes.

Named after one of the table's original developers, Dr. Alan Partin of Johns Hopkins University, the Partin Tables were created by evaluating the

---

TABLE 3.3   What's My Risk Group?

This table shows the three most commonly used classifications for low-, intermediate-, and high-risk groups. The name at the top of the column indicates the individual and/or the organization(s) that created these definitions.

	D'Amico / Harvard	Mt. Sinai	Seattle Prostate Institute / Memorial Sloan-Kettering
Low	T1–T2a PSA ≤ 10.0 Gleason 2–6	T1–T2a PSA ≤ 10.0 Gleason 2–6	T1–T2b PSA ≤ 10.0 Gleason 2–6
Intermediate	T2b and/or PSA 10.1–20.0 and/or Gleason 7	T2b or PSA 10.1–20.0 or Gleason = 7	T2c–T3 or PSA > 10.0 and/or Gleason ≥ 7
High	T2c and/or PSA > 20 and/or Gleason 8–10	T2c–T3 and/or PSA > 20 and/or Gleason 8–10. Or two of the three intermediate risk factors	Two or three of the intermediate risk factors

pathology results from radical prostatectomy patients and comparing the results with the preoperative PSA levels, Gleason scores, and stage. Based on this information, the likelihood of spread into and through the edge of the capsule, into the seminal vesicles, or into the pelvic lymph nodes was determined for individual groups of patients. (Note that other reputable groups have developed similar tools providing comparable information.)

The Partin Tables can be a useful starting point when considering treatment options, but they do not predict cure. Their aim is to take an educated guess about whether the cancer is completely confined to the prostate or if it's spread to or through the capsule, reached into the seminal vesicles, or extended to the nearby lymph nodes. Neither do the tables predict this with 100 percent accuracy for any individual patient. The tables just give the likelihood based on information from a large group of patients.

The Partin Tables also do not predict for disease outside of the surgical margin or the margin of the radioactive implant. (When the prostate is removed, the surgeon will often take an extra bit of tissue—a margin—from around the prostate. In radioactive seed implants, the margin is an area of tissue, about 5 to 10 millimeters, beyond the gland that the radiation also reaches.)

The Partin Tables don't take into account all of the factors that may predict the extent of tumor. Here's an example: Let's say we have two patients, both with a Gleason 6 cancer, stage T1c, and a PSA of 8.0 ng/mL. One patient has 7 out of 10 cores that are positive for cancer, while the other patient has only 1 out of 10 positive cores. The patient with the seven positive cores probably has a high likelihood of cancer spread beyond the capsule. Knowing the possibility of any or all of the above may impact treatment recommendation(s).

4

What Part Do Spouses and Partners Play?

Jeff M. Michalski, M.D.; John E. Sylvester, M.D.

A MAN FIGHTS prostate cancer alone, but he usually enters the battle accompanied by interested and concerned loved ones. To use the words of one spouse, "He got the diagnosis, but we both have prostate cancer." That simple statement is one of the best we've heard about how difficult prostate cancer can be for the spouse. The spouse often acts as the most significant supporter throughout the entire process of diagnosis, treatment, and healing.

We acknowledge that the diagnosis can come down like a ton of bricks. You both suddenly have to learn about the disease and the technical issues and figure out the meaning of the medical jargon. You will be learning as much about prostate cancer in a very short period as some physicians take months or years to learn.

It's normal to feel overwhelmed. You're not only trying to be a good mate, you're also trying to understand what he's going through and help him make decisions. You're trying to be the student, spouse, and friend. All of these roles cannot co-exist without some stress. Our intent in this chapter is to answer questions that you might be asking yourself and provide advice to help get you through a very taxing time.

Each patient and situation is different. Although we talk about some of the emotional difficulties that prostate cancer treatment might bring, we are also fully aware that many men and their mates navigate this illness relatively free of anxiety. No matter where you fall in this continuum, if one or both of you need assistance, we encourage you to seek support so you both can maintain equilibrium during all stages of treatment, recovery, and healing.

I know I'm supposed to "be there" to help him throughout this ordeal, but I'm feeling bewildered. How normal is this?

These feelings are very normal. It's just as normal not to feel this way. There is a spectrum of reactions because everybody adjusts to illness, both their own and a family member's, differently. The first few weeks following diagnosis can be the most difficult time, emotionally, of the whole experience. Feelings change quickly—even hour to hour. It's not uncommon to experience denial, fear, guilt, anxiety, and even loneliness.

At times I find myself angry that he has prostate cancer. Then I feel guilty about being mad. Am I crazy?

No, you're not crazy. Anger is not an uncommon reaction. Some people vent anxiety by focusing on something to blame—events or people. This might sound like, "I'm angry they didn't do a prostate specific antigen [PSA] sooner. I'm angry that they didn't do a rectal exam sooner. I'm angry that the pathologist didn't interpret the slides correctly. I'm angry that we've had to wait three months for a consultation with you."

So, our advice is that if you (or the patient) is feeling angry, tell your doctor what you're angry about. As you talk with your physician, you'll likely find that you had no control over the things you're mad about. As physicians, it's our job to help you avoid second-guessing the past so you can deal with the present and the future.

Also, we sometimes hear a lot of "what-if" questions: "What if this had been caught earlier? What if we had come to see this doctor first instead of that doctor?" When you get into "what-if" thinking, you can end up blaming yourself or taking responsibility for circumstances over which you had no control.

In Her Words

K. T. Melson was just age 48 when she learned her 59-year-old husband had cancer. They had been married for two years. Her husband did not want anyone to know about his cancer. Mrs. Melson struggled with fear, sadness, and a sense of isolation, yet quickly discovered ways to take care of herself while helping her spouse.

"When I found out my husband had cancer, I was sad. My husband was very stoic, though. He said, 'Well you know, it's early stage, and I think we're okay.' But I was crumbling inside.

"I did a lot of the treatment research. I got very confused and frustrated. There were moments where I sat by myself and went hysterical. I was trying to get as involved as I could to make things easier for him. I think sometimes, as the partner, you can't always make it so easy. You can't face it for him.

"I took the biopsy slides to a friend who's a radiation oncologist. Talking with him really calmed me down. He kept telling me, 'I need you to hear this is early stage versus hearing the word *cancer*.' That helped because I had focused on the word *cancer*, like so many of us do.

"I was also sad because my husband was so private about his illness. I couldn't go to a support group because he was afraid that someone we were acquainted with might be there. I eventually confided in girlfriends on the West Coast he didn't know. Talking with them allowed me to become a stronger caretaker.

"Besides talking to close friends, I turned to the Internet. There's a whole prostate cancer community out there. The Internet isn't ideal for everyone, but it worked in my situation.

"Go to support groups if you can. Get a lot of exercise. Try to laugh every day. Take care of yourself. Watch what you eat. Try to find ways to take naps if you're not getting a full night's sleep.

"I kept a journal of everything that happened. I wrote down how I felt—every time I was depressed or scared, I would write that in there. I also kept track of the medical information. After treatment, I wrote down how my husband was responding. I kept day-by-day descriptions of how he was feeling and improving.

"The journal also turned into a chronicle of our relationship. We were married for just two years before my husband was diagnosed. I was angry and sad, and yet I learned how to cope. His illness fast-forwarded our marriage. We learned how to communicate and re-learned the dance of how to be a couple."

What can I do to combat my own feelings of fear and my sense of being overwhelmed?

It is important to take care of yourself. If you don't, you can't take care of him. Part of taking care of yourself means communicating. Let your spouse know that you're overwhelmed. Sometimes, couples don't talk about this. This can be hard on the spouse who needs this level of communication in order to stay balanced. If your mate won't listen to you, find a friend or colleague to talk to. Ask your doctor if there are support groups for spouses of prostate cancer patients. There are a lot of advantages to being in a support group, such as reducing the sense of being isolated, gaining additional information, learning new coping skills, lessening the sense of helplessness, and providing a place where powerful emotions are shared. If a support group isn't for you, inquire if there's a social worker, psychologist, or psychiatrist your doctor can recommend.

I'm concerned that my husband is so overwhelmed that he might not hear all of the information and instructions his doctors give him at each appointment. Should I go with him to his appointments to be an "extra set of ears"?

We think it is a great idea that spouses or significant friends go to the first meetings with the doctor. Sometimes adult children of a patient will accompany their father to the consultation to provide moral support and contribute to the family's memory of the encounter. Prior to the first consultation, patients and their significant others usually know at least a little bit about prostate cancer. Sometimes, though, the information they have is incorrect. We spend a fair amount of time these days correcting misinformation and describing a lot of the technical details to our patients, so it's helpful to have both partners there to hear the information and ask questions.

While taking notes for every visit is probably not necessary, it doesn't hurt to take notes at the first few meetings. Also, ask your physician for educational materials. Many of us try to make sure that everything we tell the patient is also written somewhere—such as on consent forms and the like.

If you have specific questions you want answered, write them down and ask the doctor. Most physicians appreciate it when a patient and/or spouse is organized enough to have thought through their questions and have them written down.

In Her Words

Sophia Nelson, a Virginia resident married to her high school sweetheart for 40 years, had an inkling something was wrong when her husband's doctor called about the biopsy report. Mrs. Nelson was by her husband's side through two different treatments and unexpected side effects. She also kept track of numerous details. She offers some sage advice for others who are facing the same situation.

"I would recommend under every circumstance that the wife go with her husband when he is getting any of these results, because if the biopsy shows cancer, that's all he's going to hear. You're an extra pair of ears.

"After the diagnosis, my husband spent the next week calling everyone he could think of to get information about treatment. He did the research, and our sharing came by talking about it.

"He had his first treatment here in Virginia and the second treatment in a different city across the country. I was with him through all of this. About five days after his second treatment, he started having some painful side effects that eventually required several different medications. I took care of giving him all his medications. I curtailed a lot of my activities so that I could be there. It's such a short time in your lifetime to do that. I kept a log of what I gave him and when. This is something I definitely recommend.

"We told our children, who are grown, about his treatment. I think that when you're dealing with cancer you never know what the outcome is going to be. Never try to go through it by yourself. Tell your family. You don't need to go into all of the details. But you certainly have to inform them, and you have to tell them that this or that could happen.

"We also told friends. I go regularly to a small ministry group. They knew he had cancer, but I wouldn't go into a lot of detail about his situation. All I would say is, 'We need to pray for my husband tonight.' So, in that way I did have a chance to talk to others about it. That helped a tremendous amount.

"I'm not the kind who keeps journals, but through this I did. Sometimes I'd just put, 'good day,' and other days I'd write, 'horrible day' with this huge frown and then all the medications that he took that day. I also kept track of the expenses and insurance papers. Again, something I definitely recommend doing.

"My advice? Listen to your loved one. Listen to him and try to bring out his feelings if you can. Bring out how he's feeling about the cancer, if he's frustrated, if he's nervous, if he's afraid. If he's hurting, let him talk about it. Value what he's saying."

I understand why my husband is concerned about his cancer. So am I. But he seems almost obsessed. Is there anything I can do to help him?

Some patients deal with their disease by making it their science project. They pursue Internet information, track their PSAs with graph paper, and check and double-check everything. This is perfectly OK. This can help some patients deal with the disease, understand and come to grips with the treatment. We wouldn't discourage it unless it becomes a barrier to making a decision. Each person has to come to their own understanding in their own way and time. Don't let your research get in the way of making your choice about therapy. Sometimes the worst decision you make about your treatment is *indecision*!

Part II

TREATMENT
OPTIONS

5

Is Watchful Waiting the Same as Doing Nothing?

Brian J. Davis, M.D., Ph.D.; J. Brantley Thrasher, M.D.;
John C. Blasko, M.D.

WATCHFUL WAITING, AS the name implies, is the alternative of monitoring prostate cancer and postponing therapy—perhaps temporarily, perhaps permanently. Throughout this chapter, we'll refer to this option as *watchful waiting* but other doctors might call it by different names, including *expectant management, conservative management, observation,* or *surveillance.*

There are some very interesting survival statistics about watchful waiting. In a large population-based study of overall survival of men aged 50–79 treated by various methods, the 10-year prostate cancer specific survival rate for men with grade 1 cancer was 93 percent after conservative management, 94 percent following prostatectomy, and 90 percent after external beam radiation.[4] And, authors of a commentary that appeared in *Journal of the National Cancer Institute* note that large population-based studies show that the 15-year survival rate for appropriately selected men who are on watchful waiting is similar to the survival rate of men in the same age range who do not have prostate cancer.[5]

Although there are studies showing that men are unlikely to die from their prostate cancer if it is initially untreated, they do not tell you whether a man may have suffered as it progressed. Treatment at the time of cancer progression may slow the cancer enough that he dies of some other cause. But just because a man did not die of his prostate cancer doesn't mean he never suffered from it.

This chapter discusses the advantages and disadvantages of watchful waiting, the factors in recommending watchful waiting, and the circumstances under which treatment should be considered.

Watchful Waiting

Isn't watchful waiting just really "doing nothing"?
No. Simply because a patient's prostate cancer is not being treated doesn't mean it's being ignored. Watchful waiting is *active* surveillance. It's a way for the patient and his physician to get a sense of how rapidly the disease is, or is not, progressing. Regular prostate specific antigen (PSA) tests and digital rectal exams (DREs) are the standard methods to monitor the disease, but occasionally physicians may recommend repeat biopsies or other tests periodically to check if the cancer is progressing.

Why can watchful waiting be a good choice for some patients and a poor choice for others?
There are several reasons you might choose watchful waiting. One of the strongest motivators for this choice is the chance to avoid the possible side effects of available treatments. Two of the most common and bothersome side effects are incontinence and erectile dysfunction (ED). Concern about developing one or both of these side effects is understandable, since the prostate lies in the middle of critical junctions for sexual and urinary functions. Each of the current treatment options can affect these functions at different rates and in different ways depending on the therapy, the doctor's skill, and the patient.

Let's walk through an example of how and why a man would settle on watchful waiting. Assume that an 81-year-old man diagnosed with early stage prostate cancer is contemplating watchful waiting. His doctor determines that his cancer is not aggressive and that he has reliable urinary control but is unable to achieve a good erection. This patient also experiences other health problems, including type 2 diabetes and cardiovascular problems. Given that he might not live 10 more years (the benchmark doctors use in determining whether a patient will benefit from treatment) and the poor condition of his overall health, watchful waiting could be a solid choice because it would preserve his current quality of life, including the existing good urinary function.

What if during his remaining years the cancer progresses to the point of needing treatment? He then faces the prospect of more aggressive treatment with a lower chance of success (and a higher chance of side effects) than he would experience if he were to get immediate treatment.

After careful thought, this patient and his doctor agreed that watchful waiting would be a reasonable approach. Many prostate cancers grow so slowly that the disease can be monitored with regular PSA tests and DREs, and they may never progress to give the patient any problems. It is important to note that more aggressive cancers (those with higher Gleason scores) are usually not good candidates for watchful waiting. Even in older men, the cancer cells can spread and cause symptoms in just a few years. Ordinarily the best candidates for watchful waiting are patients whose Gleason scores are less than or equal to 6. Cancer that is scored Gleason 8 to 10 almost always needs treatment, and Gleason 7 prostate cancer falls in between.

In our 81-year-old's case, his doctor's concern about preexisting health conditions outweighed the need for immediate prostate cancer treatment. The doctor recommended, and the patient agreed, that he would get a PSA test every three months and a repeat biopsy in one year. They also agreed that during monitoring, if the patient's cancer was clearly progressing, then they would revisit the possibility of treatment.

Monitoring with PSA during watchful waiting is simple, but it must be done frequently enough to check if the cancer is progressing rapidly. So, that's a downside of watchful waiting: the patient has to commit to a lot of visits to the doctor and repeated testing.

When is watchful waiting a good choice?

The patient and his doctor weigh several factors in choosing watchful waiting. The first is overall health. If the patient is too ill to benefit from cancer treatment, he might be a candidate for watchful waiting. For example, if a patient has suffered multiple heart attacks and still has an unstable heart when he's diagnosed with low-grade, low-stage prostate cancer, he may choose watchful waiting until his condition improves.

There is no hard-and-fast rule about how old a patient has to be in order to contemplate watchful waiting, but age is another consideration. Generally, men younger than 65 have a relatively long life expectancy and are more likely to have the prostate cancer progress during their lifetimes. Men in this age bracket usually select a curative treatment. However, patients in their early 80s with low-grade tumors and low PSAs often consider watchful waiting as an option because of this age group's shorter life expectancy.

The tumor grade and stage are the third and fourth factors. Older men with low-grade and low-stage tumors are the best candidates for watchful waiting.

Another aspect of watchful waiting pertains to the psychology of having cancer. One of the difficulties with watchful waiting is the knowledge that a cancer is present but whether it is progressing may be unknown to both the doctor and the patient. Frequent visits and assurances from the doctor can help alleviate this fear of the unknown. But, in truth, watchful waiting has been difficult for some of our patients—especially those who tend to focus on and think about their cancer daily. It is these patients who find watchful waiting to be a burden, and each trip to the doctor becomes an anxiety-filled experience. If watchful waiting is significantly affecting the quality of a patient's emotional and mental well-being, then it may be time to consider treatment.

Can I use my PSA score alone to tell me if I'm a good candidate for watchful waiting?

No. While the PSA value typically measures the status of the cancer, we cannot rely on it completely. For one thing, PSA levels can be influenced by prostate conditions other than cancer (see Chapter 1). Also, high-grade tumors may produce PSA at a very low level. Many factors—stage, grade of the tumor, and the number of positive biopsies, as well as the PSA—should weigh into the decision for or against watchful waiting.

How frequently should I be examined during watchful waiting?

In most instances, patients see their doctors at least every six months. In the early stages after diagnosis, it may be appropriate to visit the physician more frequently, perhaps every three months. While most watchful waiting patients see their doctors twice a year, our best advice is for each patient to work closely with his own doctor to establish a suitable schedule.

What are the advantages of watchful waiting?

The chief advantage is that patients who qualify for watchful waiting can delay or entirely avoid side effects from treatment. Patients who are elderly, who have serious medical conditions, and/or who are sexually active may choose watchful waiting because of their desire to maintain their current quality of life for several more years before treatment is necessary. What's more, if a patient makes positive lifestyle changes—getting more exercise, decreasing saturated fats, avoiding excessive calories, and incorporating more fruits and vegetables into his diet—he'll enhance his health. That can add to his overall well-being during the months (or years) of watchful waiting.

What are the disadvantages of watchful waiting?

Occasionally, the tumor progresses rapidly. There are also uncommon cases in which the patient is not monitored carefully and the tumor advances to a higher stage or grade. Tumors that become larger may require more aggressive treatment and, consequently, a greater number and higher degree of side effects, plus a possibility of the treatment being less effective.

The physician will employ all of his or her experience and use the best testing technology in making an estimate of the cancer's aggressiveness. Usually, the estimate is right. But it's impossible for any physician to predict with 100 percent accuracy if or how rapidly a cancer will progress.

If I am on watchful waiting, how will I know when treatment should be reconsidered?

This is difficult to answer. Again, it's patient-specific. If the PSA rises above 10 ng/mL (and certainly 20 ng/mL) the cancer is less likely to be confined just to the prostate. If the PSA increases to these levels during watchful waiting, we will probably ask the patient to consider treatment, even if he is of advanced age or has other health conditions. The rate of rise of PSA may also influence the decision to reconsider treatment, but there are no widely accepted standards.

A change in Gleason score is another factor that favors treatment. If a cancer was Gleason 5 but a repeat biopsy revealed a change to Gleason 7 or higher, this data might prompt us to recommend a new course of action.

Even with a rising PSA, an increased Gleason score, or a new nodule felt during a DRE, the patient may still decide to decline treatment. It is valuable for the patient and his physician to agree on the point at which treatment should be considered. That's why we cannot overemphasize the need for each patient to develop a trusting relationship with his doctor and work closely with him or her during the watchful waiting program to determine when, or if, to seek curative therapy.

6

Should I Have My Prostate Removed?

J. Brantley Thrasher, M.D.; John P. Mulhall, M.D.;
Brian J. Davis, M.D., Ph.D.; Mack Roach III, M.D.;
John E. Sylvester, M.D.

REMOVING THE PROSTATE (the technical term is *prostatectomy*) has been a mainstay of prostate cancer treatment since the early 1900s. That's when Dr. Hugh Hampton Young at Johns Hopkins Hospital started removing the prostate through an incision between the scrotum and the anus. It wasn't until the 1940s that surgeons began removing the prostate through an abdominal incision. But one of the problems with these early approaches was excessive blood loss.

It wasn't until the 1970s that surgeons, again at Johns Hopkins, solved this dilemma. They were the first to tie off the major veins of the prostate and bladder to stem the disproportionate blood flow. Less blood in the surgical field meant they had an improved view of what they were doing. Patients began to fare better immediately. The 1980s brought another improvement when surgeons introduced the nerve-sparing prostatectomy.

Since these two developments—better blood control and the ability to spare nerves responsible for erection—prostatectomies have had a resurgence in popularity as a treatment for prostate cancer. In this chapter, we take a close look at what happens during surgery, the side effects, and other considerations so you can talk with your own doctor about whether it's right for you.

Radical Prostatectomy Options

I have heard there are a couple of different ways to remove the prostate. What are they?

The most common ways to remove the prostate are the radical retropubic, perineal, and laparoscopic techniques. The radical retropubic approach—so named because the prostate lies behind the pubic bone—requires a large abdominal incision (see Figure 6.1).

During the delicate operation, the surgeon may remove a sample of the pelvic lymph nodes and send them to a pathologist for an immediate preliminary evaluation. If the nodes are cancerous, often the surgeon will stop the procedure and not remove the prostate. This is because the cancer has already spread to the nodes, and most evidence suggests that removing the prostate when the cancer has spread to the lymph nodes will do no good in

---

FIGURE 6.1   Radical Retropubic Prostatectomy

This is the surgical position of a man undergoing a radical retropubic prostatectomy. This method of removing the prostate requires a single abdominal incision.

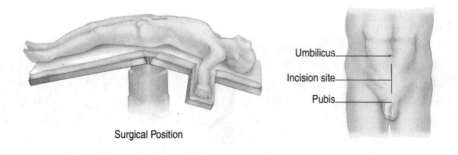

achieving a cure. (The primary treatment option for patients with positive nodes is immediate and continuous hormonal therapy.)

If the lymph nodes are not cancerous, the surgical team continues its precise task of removing the prostate, the portion of urethra contained within the prostate, the seminal vesicles, and the vas deferens from the surrounding tissue. The final step is reattaching the bladder to the urethra.

What is a perineal prostatectomy?

With this technique, the surgeon makes the incision between the anus and the scrotum (see Figure 6.2). The advantage of perineal prostatectomy compared to retropubic surgery is that patients tend to experience less blood loss, less trauma to the body, and less pain, and they heal somewhat faster. Most patients go home in one to two days. However, one downside of per-

---

FIGURE 6.2   Radical Perineal Prostatectomy

In a perineal prostatectomy, the patient's legs are put into stirrups so the area between the anus and scrotum is easily accessed. One incision is made to remove the prostate.

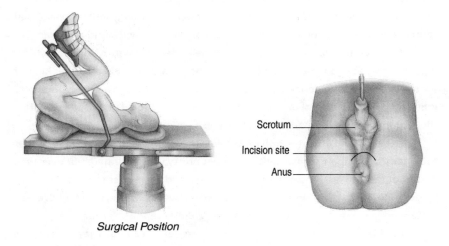

Scrotum

Incision site

Anus

Surgical Position

ineal prostatectomy is that it's next to impossible to remove pelvic lymph nodes for testing. If the surgeon wants to evaluate the lymph nodes during a perineal prostatectomy, he or she must make another incision in the abdomen. Fortunately, the majority of contemporary patients have less than 1 percent chance of positive lymph node involvement, making the perineal approach acceptable.

In His Words

At age 59, Larry Bly didn't have any idea that he was harboring prostate cancer. Semiretired from the construction industry and living in the Kansas City area, Mr. Bly's life was full of physical activity and travel. An annual physical led to the discovery of prostate cancer.

"When I went for my annual physical in 2000, I told my doctor that I wanted a PSA [prostate specific antigen] test taken. He gave me a rectal exam and he felt a bump. He sent me to a urologist. The biopsy came back that it was malignant. My Gleason scale was 2 + 3. My PSA was 4.6.

"I knew nothing about prostate cancer. My wife's brother is a nurse and I asked him about it. He sent me a pamphlet. I knew of a young lady studying down at the University of Kansas Medical Center. She gave me a book about prostate cancer.

"I asked another friend of mine who worked in a urology lab at the KU med center if he knew a good surgeon. He did, and that's how I found my urologist. When I met with him, I asked him about the different kinds of prostatectomy because of what I had read in the book. My doctor said he could do either kind of surgery. But I read the perineal prostatectomy had less blood loss and the recovery is quicker. So I went with that. I scheduled it as quick as I could get in. The day after the surgery I was walking and I went home in a couple of days.

"I leaked urine at first, which I was told would happen. I wore a pad for about four months. For the first month it would get pretty well saturated, but over time it just got less and less. Today, if I'm sitting down and I lean over to get something, I'll get in the right position and I will leak some. But it's not very bad. I have had some change in erectile function since surgery. But I use shots for that.

"My PSA has not elevated. They can't even get a reading. They say that it's really not detectable. My experience with this procedure was super good, and I think it goes right back to your doctor."

What is a laparoscopic prostatectomy?

A laparoscope is a slender, tubelike instrument that allows the surgeon to see into small areas and perform surgery. Instead of making a single, long abdominal incision, the urologist makes several small ones (see Figure 6.3) and uses the laparoscope and other instruments to remove the prostate. The chief advantages of laparoscopic prostatectomies are quicker recovery and less abdominal pain compared with a standard radical prostatectomy. Laparoscopic prostatectomies are difficult, though, and surgeons must perform many cases before they develop enough skill to do the procedure efficiently and with the fewest possible side effects. Moreover, it will be several years before we know the scientific results and advantages of laparoscopic radical prostatectomy. Little is published regarding the likelihood that the laparoscopic approach will remove all the cancer and result in the same 10-year disease control rates that standard radical prostatectomy or radiation therapy achieves.

FIGURE 6.3   Laparoscopic Prostatectomy

For a laparoscopic prostatectomy, the surgeon makes several small incisions in the abdominal area through which slender instruments are inserted to excise and remove the gland.

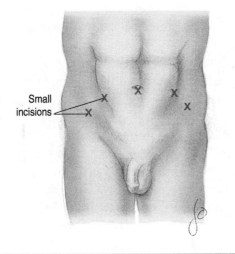

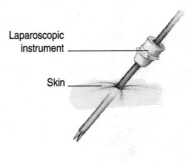

What is nerve-sparing surgery?

Neurovascular bundles lie on both sides of the prostate, just outside of the capsule. In select patients with small cancers, urologists leave one or both of these bundles intact in hopes of maintaining erectile function.

Not every patient who chooses a radical prostatectomy is a good candidate for the nerve-sparing procedure, though. It's most effective in men with only the smallest of tumors. Men with large tumors or cancer in both prostate lobes are generally poor candidates for nerve-sparing surgery. Larger tumors have a greater risk of having positive margins. (A surgical margin simply means the edges of the tissue. When the prostate is sent to the lab for tests, one of the things the pathologist looks for is whether cancer cells are on the edge of the cut tissue. A positive surgical margin means that cancer is found at the margin—or edge—of the specimen. A negative margin means the cancer was likely contained entirely within the prostate.)

A man with cancer at the apex of the prostate is also a poor candidate for nerve-sparing surgery. Similarly, a patient who is already experiencing erectile dysfunction is discouraged from the nerve-sparing operation. In this case, the nerve-sparing procedure is not going to increase this man's chance of having erections.

Even if everything looks good for a nerve-sparing surgery and the patient and his surgeon choose this option, it's only during the operation—once the surgeon sees the tumor's extent—that he or she will make the final decision whether to leave one or both neurovascular bundles intact. Also, maintaining erectile function not only depends on maintaining the integrity of the nerves responsible for an erection, but also the blood supply to and from the penis. The prostatectomy might alter the patient's blood supply so that even if his nerves were kept, he still might not be able to have erections.

Is every urologist capable of using the nerve-sparing surgical technique?

No. Although urologists are capable of *trying* to do it, not every urologist is equally capable of implementing it with high rates of success. Should you want to know if the surgeon you're considering can perform nerve-sparing surgeries, one way to ask this question is, "Did you receive training to perform nerve-sparing radical prostatectomies, and how often is erectile function maintained after you perform the surgery?"

What is a sural nerve graft?

A sural nerve graft is performed during a radical prostatectomy. The surgeon detaches a portion of the sural nerve from the patient's lower leg, near the ankle, and grafts this in place of the removed erectile nerves. Sural nerve grafts are primarily used for men whose surgeons deliberately excise (remove) the nerves because of extent of the tumor.

Preliminary data shows that grafting a nerve may improve erectile function, but there's a great deal of debate about whether this is effective. The procedure has been around for only a few years, it's not performed routinely, and studies so far have focused only on a small number of patients.

There are a few downsides to a sural nerve graft. It adds about 45 minutes to a radical prostatectomy, so the patient has to be under anesthesia for that much longer. A second incision, this one on the leg, must also heal. The man will also lose sensation in a small area on the outside of the foot.

How soon can I go back to work after a prostatectomy?

Patients spend up to three days in the hospital before going home. While some studies show that patients can get back to work in several days, usually it's at least a couple of weeks before they're back on the job. An important determinant is the type of job the patient has and the type of prostatectomy he undergoes. For instance, a patient in one of our practices was a banker who wanted to have his surgery on a Thursday and wished to be back on the job Monday morning. His was an unusual request, and after a great deal of consultation and counseling, the patient opted for a perineal prostatectomy. Indeed, he was back on the job three full days later. Bear in mind, however, that he was an executive in a comparatively nonphysical profession who sat in meetings much of the day.

For a man who has a much more physical job, his back-to-work story will be different—even with a perineal prostatectomy. The incision needs four to six weeks to heal before the patient can put physical stress on it. So, men in physically challenging professions are likely to be off work longer before they can resume their usual posts.

How safe is it for me to travel to a "center of excellence" far away from my area for surgery? If so, when can I return home?
Traveling to a highly regarded center for the surgery usually is not a problem, nor is traveling back home. The patient's hometown physician usually conducts the follow-up of removing the catheter, checking the incision, and conducting the needed postsurgical tests, such as PSA.

What Is Prostate Cryosurgery?

Cryo means "cold." Most simply, prostate cryosurgery relies on rapid freezing and thawing to destroy cancer cells. This procedure is also called cryotherapy and cryoablation (*ablation* is defined as destroying the function of a tissue). Unlike a radical prostatectomy, which is the complete removal of the prostate, cryosurgery destroys the prostate and a rim of surrounding tissue while the gland is still in the body.

After the patient receives anesthesia, the surgeon inserts a device into the bladder and urethra to prevent them from freezing. Next, the surgeon places an ultrasound probe in the rectum. This helps guide the placement of several cryo probes through the perineum and into the prostate. Super-cold gas, either argon or nitrogen, circulates through the probes. The gas causes the tips of the probe to become extremely cold and freeze the prostate tissue. In some centers, the prostate thaws for about 30 minutes before the surgeon applies a second treatment. Early studies indicate that this second round may do a more thorough job of killing larger amounts of tissue.

The patient can go home the same day and his catheter is left in place for some time. The reports of pain are minimal, and doctors begin monitoring the PSA level beginning at six months.

Although advances in the technique have reduced the rates of incontinence over the past few years, erectile dysfunction (ED) continues to be a problem. The procedure freezes the neurovascular bundles that control erection, which means a high level of ED in patients who undergo cryosurgery.

Also, the urethra is warmed during cryosurgery. One concern is that studies show more than 17 percent of patients have prostate cancers that involve the urethra and more than 34 percent of patients have cancer within a few millimeters of the urethra. Warming the urethra might allow cancer cells near the urethra to survive.

Other serious injuries to the bladder and rectum can also occur. There is no evidence yet that this treatment is superior to surgery or radiation therapy.

Important Considerations for Radical Prostatectomy

What are the advantages of a radical prostatectomy?
This approach can indeed cure prostate cancer. For most patients, the cure rates of radical prostatectomy are comparable to other approaches, particularly radiation therapy.

Many patients choose prostatectomy because of a desire "to have it all out now"—they want to get the cancer-harboring organ out of their bodies (which surgery does in the majority of cases). Another potential advantage is that because the removed prostate is examined by a pathologist, the extent of the cancer can be determined. This postsurgical pathological examination allows for the recommendation of additional treatments if needed.

Which patients are good candidates for surgery?
The general rule is that patients need to experience 10 years of benefit from the operation. If a man is first diagnosed with low-grade prostate cancer at age 82, chances are that within 10 years he will die of something other than his prostate cancer. So, given the serious potential for side effects and complications, the doctor of this 82-year-old patient might counsel him to avoid surgery and begin watchful waiting or seek a less invasive treatment. On the other hand, if a 62-year-old man has prostate cancer and is in otherwise good health, surgery could be a fine option due to his comparatively long life expectancy.

When is surgery a poor treatment choice?
Surgery is not a very good choice when patients are a poor operative risk because of other health problems. The most significant factors for predicting success are age and overall health. The major factor precluding surgery is if the patient's life expectancy is less than 10 years; patients over 75 years old are generally not considered for radical prostatectomy. Health factors affecting tolerance to a major surgery must also be considered. Obesity is a factor in whether or not radical retropubic prostatectomies can be performed, but obesity is not generally a problem in radical perineal or laparoscopic prostatectomies.

What are the risks?

Any major surgery carries risk. If you're thinking about surgery (or any other treatment, for that matter), your job is to work with your physician to figure out if the potential benefits outweigh the possible risks.

In radical prostatectomy, damage to the bladder and the rectum can occur. The patient may experience adverse reactions to anesthesia or other medications. Life-threatening trouble with major organs (such as the heart and/or the kidneys) during surgery can also take place, especially if those organs are already weak from existing disease—but this is infrequent.

Death can occur, though it is very rare. Each year in the United States, between 0.1 percent and 0.7 percent of patients die during radical retropubic prostatectomies.[6] It appears that risk of mortality is associated with age. Figures show that the death rate from prostatectomy in men 65–75 years old is less than 1 percent, but in men older than 80 the mortality rate nears 5 percent.[7] Blood loss is often minimal and transfusion rates have fallen over the years. For example, at one of our institutions less than 5 percent of patients require transfusion for retropubic prostatectomies, and for prostates removed through the perineum, the rate of requiring transfusion is less than 1 percent.

Which operation should I have?

There are a couple of advantages to retropubic radical prostatectomies compared to other approaches, including the ability to remove a few lymph nodes to test for cancer and possibly leaving one or both of the nerve bundles.

Another primary advantage with radical retropubic prostatectomy is that surgeons are often able to remove more tissue, which means a greater chance of removing all of the cancer. (In cases where positive surgical margins remain after surgery, additional therapy including radiation therapy, hormonal therapy, or both, may be considered.)

In terms of advantages for radical perineal prostatectomies, patients have less blood loss and tend to recover quicker. Most comparative studies show that radical perineal prostatectomy has similar cancer control compared to radical retropubic prostatectomy. Continence and potency data between the two are also the same. A nerve-sparing technique can also be done with a radical retropubic or a laparoscopic prostatectomy.

Can patients with advanced prostate cancer undergo surgery?

When the cancer has extended past the prostate, there's less chance of successful treatment with a single therapy, including surgery. *However*, there is a small group of surgeons who offer surgery on an otherwise healthy patient with locally advanced prostate cancer, and even in patients with high risk of lymph node involvement. This is a controversial practice, but there is some limited experience in doing surgery on advanced prostate cancer.

Note that most patients with locally advanced, nonmetastatic prostate cancer undergo external beam radiation therapy plus hormonal therapy.

What is the most desirable PSA value following surgery?

The PSA should fall to a nearly undetectable level following surgery; most surgeons look for a level of 0.2 ng/mL or lower. Some data suggests that having detectable PSA after a radical prostatectomy indicates a higher likelihood of treatment failure.

In men who have had a radical prostatectomy and still have a measurable PSA, where does the PSA come from?

It's possible for the urologist to leave behind small amounts of normal prostate tissue. As testosterone interacts with this normal prostate tissue, the tiny remnants of the gland might produce PSA. This small amount of benign prostate tissue should not cause the PSA to rise continually. A continually increasing PSA is usually due to recurrent cancer.

If cancer is in the lymph nodes and they are removed, does that increase my chance for cure?

The current thought is that removing lymph nodes at the time of surgery doesn't improve the cure rate. The urologist removes a small number of lymph nodes for testing only. If these lymph nodes are positive for cancer, it is likely that some of the remaining pelvic lymph nodes are involved and the cancer has spread to other parts of the body.

If the lymph nodes are positive, what next?

Typically, if the lymph nodes are positive, treatments such as hormonal therapy and sometimes external beam radiation are started. Because finding positive lymph nodes is so serious, interest is growing in using experimental protocols of chemotherapy for these patients.

The Most Common Side Effects

How often does ED occur after radical prostatectomy?

Whether a man chooses external beam radiation or radical prostatectomy, his chance of developing ED appears to be about the same—at least according to one study looking at 802 men. Sixty-nine percent of these men reported normal erectile function prior to treatment. About 50 months after treatment, 10 percent of patients who had radical prostatectomy reported normal erectile function. The news wasn't much different for radiation patients; 15 percent of men in this group reported normal functioning. On the other hand, nearly 40 percent of men who were on watchful waiting still had adequate erections six months later.[8] Other studies, however, have shown that radiation therapy is less likely than surgery to cause ED, but further research on this topic is necessary.

Erectile dysfunction frequently occurs after nerve-sparing surgeries, too. The risk of ED doesn't appear to depend on whether the surgeon saves one nerve bundle (unilateral nerve-sparing surgery) or both neurovascular bundles (bilateral nerve-sparing prostatectomy). One study asked men to fill out a questionnaire about their sexual and urinary functions before surgery and then had them answer the same questions three and 12 months later. One year later, about 80 percent of patients who had bilateral nerve-sparing surgery reported inadequate erections. Those who had unilateral nerve-sparing surgery fared about the same. This, despite the fact that patients who underwent bilateral and unilateral nerve-sparing surgeries tended to be younger and had less advanced cancers than those who had standard radical prostatectomies.[9]

Conversely, in a study out of Johns Hopkins, 86 percent of the 64 men who had bilateral nerve-sparing surgery achieved erections 18 months after surgery. About one-third of these men used Viagra. Bear in mind, however, the average age of men in this study was under 60. Age plays a big role in a return to erectile function, no matter what the treatment. The younger the patient, the better his chance of keeping erections.

In His Words

Davis Watson works 400 acres of Missouri farmland, which keeps him fit and healthy. Although Mr. Watson had no symptoms, his brother's prostate cancer diagnosis prompted Mr. Watson to get checked. Mr. Watson's PSA test came back high, and the subsequent biopsy revealed cancer. He was just 41 years old.

"My wife and I went to doctors statewide and talked to them. They pretty well advised me to have the surgery because at that time the research didn't go back as far on the seed implants.

"I found a surgeon I liked, and he decided it was best to have the kind of surgery that goes through the abdomen. I did have a lot of abdominal cramping and pain for the two and a half days I was in the hospital.

"My doctor took the catheter out after three weeks. He told me I could start doing some light-duty work. I started very slow and worked my way back into what I used to do. Between nine and 10 weeks, I was going strong.

"Just after the operation, I leaked urine. My doctor warned me that it could take three months, sometimes a year, before things are right. I wore Depends for four or five days. I didn't have to after that, but I did leak some when I bent over or picked stuff up. But it got better little by little. In a few months, I was doing great.

"As far as the sexual part, I'm doing well. My doctor said that for some people it takes a year, sometimes two. But he thought I'd be fine because of my age. Within probably seven or eight months things were getting very good. I'm back to normal and don't take medication to get an erection.

"If I were older, I wouldn't want to have this surgery because of the soreness, the healing process. It's a pretty tough go.

"I know there's all different ideas and treatments, but I think I got the best treatment for me. I also think belief in your doctor and following instructions thoroughly aids in the healing process."

Can anything be done to help retain erectile function after surgery?
There's a concept called penile rehabilitation, the goal of which is to maintain the health of the erection tissue. If the erection tissue remains healthy while the nerves are healing, the patient has a better chance of regaining erections.

It doesn't matter if patients get erections with the use of pills, shots, or other methods. The important point is to stretch the erectile tissue of the penis to keep it healthy. If a man's arm was immobilized in a cast for six months, would he expect it to be able to lift anything after the cast was removed? No. It's the same idea with erection tissue. It must be exercised to maintain its ability. Penile rehabilitation does not promote nerve growth. It keeps normal tissue healthy during the time of possible nerve regeneration after surgery.

We recommend that men achieve at least two to three erections per week after any of the treatments, including surgery, and that they begin as soon as possible. Even men who don't have the nerve-sparing surgery are put on penile rehabilitation. This is because in a small percentage of non-nerve-sparing prostatectomies, a small amount of nerve tissue remains. Keeping even this small amount of erection tissue healthy helps preserve the ability of having erections with the assistance of the medications.

Should I start penile therapy before my radical prostatectomy?

That depends. If you routinely experience nocturnal or sex erections, there's no need to undergo penile rehabilitation in preparation for your surgery. However, if you experience poor or no erections (because of hormonal therapy, for instance), it's a good idea to begin penile rehabilitation *prior* to radical prostatectomy and maintain the effort after surgery, too. This same advice holds true for men undergoing hormone therapy to shrink the prostate prior to seed implantation. Be sure to talk with your own doctor.

How is ED treated?

Three types of therapy are available to treat ED: drug therapy, vacuum erection devices, and penile implants.

- **Drug therapy.** The most well-known oral drug is Viagra, but other similar agents are or will soon be on the market. Viagra works by enhancing an enzyme in the penis responsible for increased blood flow into the erection chambers. Viagra is taken before sexual relations, and it can be used every day, but no more than once in a 24-hour period. Viagra does not produce an erection. Sexual stimulation must be performed, and patients usually need to wait at least one hour after taking the pill before the erection can be enhanced.

All patients should talk to their doctors before using Viagra. While generally safe, some men should consider alternatives. If the patient is on nitroglycerine medications, doctors shouldn't prescribe this drug.

The second way to administer erection-giving drugs is to insert a tiny suppository about one inch into the penile urethra, where the drug dissolves. About 30 percent to 40 percent of men get an erection with this treatment. In terms of side effects, men may experience some penile pain and/or dizziness. However, the results of this therapy are inconsistent—sometimes the suppository works, sometimes it doesn't.

The third way of administering drugs is by penile injection. This technique requires injecting a medication into the penis with a tiny needle and syringe. The needle is so small that the injection feels much like a mosquito bite. Penile injection therapy is the gold standard in drug therapy because of the very high response rate. Several erection-improving drugs are in the syringe, resulting in about a 90 percent chance of getting an erection sufficient enough for penetration. The average man gets an erection within 5 to 10 minutes and achieves a 20- to 30-minute erection. (Note that this response rate is an overall figure, but there is no reason to expect radical prostatectomy patients to respond differently.) Penile injection should be undertaken only after careful training and dose adjustment guided by the urologist.

- **Vacuum erection devices.** Vacuum erection devices (VEDs) are a second-line treatment. A mechanical device is placed over the outside of the penis, and the chamber generates negative pressure—a vacuum—that pulls blood into the penis. A ring is placed at the base of the penis, which should stay in place for no more than half an hour.

  One problem with this therapy is that it's difficult to integrate into lovemaking. The ring on the man's penis is sometimes uncomfortable and is a reminder of the problem. Nor does the penis look or feel normal. Only a small percentage of patients who start out with VED are still using it a year later. As far as those who should avoid using VED, men who are on anticoagulants shouldn't use them.

- **Penile implants.** A third-line therapy is penile implant surgery. Most centers reserve this surgery for patients who have failed or are unable to tolerate the drug or vacuum therapies. There are two different types of prosthesis—one is inflated with a pump and another keeps the penis semi-rigid at all times.

As with all surgeries, complications can arise. One side effect is postoperative pain, as well as time lost from work, up to two weeks. About 15 percent of patients will need to have another operation within 10 years because the implant breaks down. In 2 percent to 3 percent of cases, the device becomes infected. This usually means a second surgery to put in a new prosthesis.

Of all ED treatment, however, penile implants have the highest satisfaction profile because of their excellent rigidity and speed of onset of erections (seconds).

At what point following radical prostatectomy can incontinence occur, and can this become a permanent problem?

There's no doubt that a man's continence is going to be different, because surgery removes a portion of the urethra responsible for some of the urinary control. Stress incontinence (leaking a few drops of urine during sneezing, coughing, or lifting heavy objects) occurs just after the catheter is removed, which is from 10 days to two weeks following surgery. After the catheter is removed, stress incontinence occurs for weeks or months simply because the remaining sphincter muscle is not yet strong enough to retain all of the urine in the bladder.

Many patients report regaining most of their continence after three months, but it can take up to a year. One year after surgery, nearly 92 percent of 593 patients treated at one center of excellence experienced complete continence, 8 percent reported mild or moderate stress incontinence, and 0.3 percent had severe incontinence.[10]

Unfortunately, not all urologists have this degree of success. In one study, 24 months after surgery 9.6 percent of men reported either having no control or often dripping or leaking urine, 13.8 percent reported leaking at least twice per day, and 28.1 percent of respondents said they wore pads to keep dry.[11]

The age at which a man undergoes radical prostatectomy plays a role in incontinence. The older the patient, the greater the chance of incontinence. The good news in all of this is that most men who participate in quality of life studies report incontinence does *not* affect their lifestyle. A patient in one of our practices, a carpenter, is a perfect example. His work requires him to lift a 40-pound toolbox many times each day. He knows that each time he tries to pick it up, the abdominal stress from the lifting could cause him to leak a few drops of urine. So, all he does is tighten his sphincter muscle before he picks up the toolbox. In his case, he found a simple solution to what could otherwise be a vexing problem. Other men wear thin absorbent pads in their underwear.

What Are Kegel Exercises?

Kegels are exercises to strengthen the muscles controlling the sphincter related to bladder control and continence. These muscles contract and relax under your command to control the opening and closing of your bladder. When they are weak, urine leakage may occur. However, through regular exercise, you can build up their strength and endurance and, in many cases, regain bladder control.

How Do I Do Kegel Exercises?

Begin by locating the muscles to be exercised. As you are urinating, try to stop or slow the urine without tensing the muscles of your legs, buttocks, or abdomen. It's important not to use these other muscles because only the pelvic floor muscles help with bladder control. Squeeze in the rectal area to tighten the anus as if trying not to pass gas; you will be using the correct muscles. When you are able to slow or stop the stream of urine, you have located the correct muscles. Feel the sensation of the muscles pulling inward and upward.

Set aside three to four times each day for exercising. Squeeze your muscles to the slow count of four. Then, relax these muscles completely to the slow count of four. This four-second contraction and four-second relaxation make one set. Complete 10 sets during each of your daily exercise sessions.

If your pelvic floor muscles are very weak, you should begin by contracting the muscles for only three to five seconds. Do the best you can and continue faithfully. In a few weeks, you should be able to increase the amount of time you are able to hold the contraction and the number of exercise sets you are able to do. Your goal is to hold each contraction for 10 seconds, to relax for 10 seconds, and to complete 25 to 30 sets.

Whether you are doing pelvic muscle exercises to improve or maintain bladder control, you must do them regularly on a lifetime basis.

How can I tell if the urologist I'm seeing has good results when performing radical prostatectomies?

An important index is to find out how frequently the urologist performs this surgery. If the surgeon is doing only one or two radical prostatectomies per month, then perhaps the patient might want to talk with another urologist to get a second opinion. In some larger institutions, we see urologists who perform approximately 100 radical prostatectomies per year. It's not a requirement that the surgeon does 100 per year, but going to a surgeon who is highly practiced means he or she is more likely to be more skilled than one who does just a couple dozen annually.

Also, don't be afraid to ask the surgeon the tough questions. Inquire about things such as their surgical complication rates, rates of injuries to nearby organs, transfusion rates, and the rates of erectile dysfunction and incontinence. A radical prostatectomy is a once-in-a-lifetime operation. If a surgeon gets upset because a patient asked about complication rates, the patient could use that as a clue to seek additional opinions.

7

How Does External Beam Radiation Therapy Work?

Brian J. Davis, M.D., Ph.D.; Mack Roach III, M.D.;
Katsuto Shinohara, M.D.; Peter D. Grimm, D.O.

DURING THE PAST 90 years, radiation for prostate cancer has evolved from an imprecise therapy into today's highly sophisticated treatments that use linear accelerators, proton beams, neutron beams, and radioactive seeds for implants.

External beam radiation came into its own as a prostate cancer treatment during the 1950s and 1960s with the introduction of cobalt therapy. Cobalt-60 radiation appeared at first to cure as many cases of prostate cancer as surgery without serious side effects. However, researchers soon found that cobalt radiation carried its own set of adverse effects. This knowledge led to the development of linear accelerators, which allowed for higher doses of radiation but with generally fewer side effects than the old cobalt-60 treatments.

The technical advances in prostate cancer radiation therapy in the last few decades have also decreased the rates of urinary incontinence, erectile dysfunction (ED), and other side effects. These advances, coupled with evidence that modern techniques appear to be as effective as prostatectomy in curing early stage prostate cancer, make radiation a convincing choice for successful prostate cancer treatment. Although precise numbers are not yet reported, it is likely that 50 percent or more of U.S. prostate cancer patients each year receive either seeds or external beam radiation therapy as part of their treatment regimen.

In this chapter we'll take a straightforward look at the different kinds of external beam radiation, what to expect during treatment, which patients are good candidates, and the possible side effects.

External Beam Basics

How does radiation kill cancer cells?

An individual cell in the human body and most other living organisms reproduces by dividing into two daughter cells. This division (the technical term is *mitosis*) is how new cells are produced for growth and repair. From the time a cell divides until it divides again is called cell cycle time. Every type of cell in the body has its own cell cycle time. For example, the cells lining the mouth have about a 48-hour cell cycle time; they replace themselves within two days. Normal, noncancerous prostate cells are not as short-lived. They have very long cell cycle times, as do some prostate cancer cells.

Radiation treatment impairs a cell's ability to undergo mitosis by damaging the cell's DNA (which is an abbreviation for its chemical name, deoxyribonucleic acid). DNA resembles a ladder. The radiation pops holes into the sides of the ladder so that after a time only the rungs are holding the ladder together. When it comes time to divide, the rungs separate just like they're supposed to, but the ladder crumbles because of the many holes in the ladder's sides. The cell dies because the DNA (in our analogy, the ladder) simply breaks into tiny pieces.

How is external beam radiation delivered?

Patients treated for prostate cancer with external radiation get daily treatments, Monday through Friday, for eight to nine weeks. This divides the total dose of radiation into small daily amounts, or fractions (which is why it's called fractionated radiation therapy). Normal prostate cells are much more effective at repairing the radiation damage to their DNA than prostate cancer cells. Thus, these smaller hits of radiation allow the noncancerous tissue to repair itself after radiation. Most cancer cells don't recover well after being hit with radiation, even when it's given in small doses such as those of fractionated radiation therapy.

I've been hearing about photon, proton, and neutron beam radiation. What are they?

Photon, proton, and neutron radiation are types of radiation that are delivered by machine. Seed implantation is also radiation but it is delivered internally (see Figure 7.1).

Low-energy photon radiation is also known as x-rays, such as a chest x-ray. The energy and amount of this radiation is low enough to penetrate

---

FIGURE 7.1   Types of Radiation Therapy for Prostate Cancer

This chart illustrates the different types of radiation used to treat prostate cancer. 3D conformal radiation and IMRT are simply different ways of delivering photon radiation. Proton and neutron radiation are completely different types of external beam radiation that use subatomic particles. Seed implants means that radioactive sources are permanently inserted into the body. Iodine-125 and palladium-103 are the two isotopes used in these implants. The other type of implant is a temporary procedure, in which iridium is inserted into the prostate for a short period and then removed.

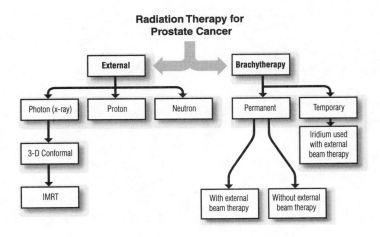

the body to create x-ray images, but it's too low to damage any significant number of cells.

High-energy photon radiation is produced by a linear accelerator, is more potent than low dose x-rays, and is capable of killing cancer. With this treatment, the patient lies on a special treatment table as the linear accelerator rotates above and around the prostate area to deliver the radiation (see Figure 7.2).

What is 3D-CRT?

The goal of three-dimensional conformal radiation therapy (3D-CRT) is to deliver a higher dose of photon radiation while preserving more of the surrounding normal tissue. Three-dimensional conformal radiation therapy uses the photon energy from a linear accelerator, but special software is used to plan and deliver the higher radiation doses with greater accuracy. This planning is applied to detailed cross-sectional images of a patient's internal

FIGURE 7.2   Linear Accelerator

As the patient lies on the treatment table of a linear accelerator, the large arm above rotates to different angles to deliver the radiation.

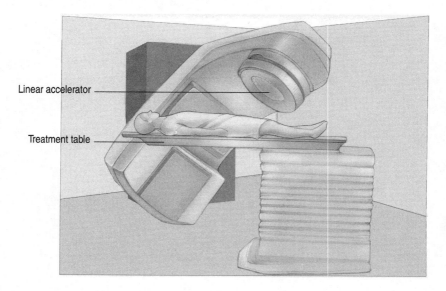

anatomy. The imaging, usually done with a CT scanner, allows for the precise identification of the prostate and normal adjacent structures, such as the rectum and bladder.

With 3D-CRT, the patient lies on a treatment table just as if he is to receive normal photon radiation, but the radiation beam in each of several fields is matched to the shape of the prostate while avoiding much nearby anatomy. This means the prostate gets the strongest dose of radiation, with less radiation striking the rectum and bladder. Virtually all radiation treatment centers in the United States use 3D-CRT, and it is estimated that within three to five years most centers will be using a more advanced form of 3D-CRT known as intensity modulated radiation therapy (IMRT), as some centers do now.

What is IMRT?

Intensity modulated radiation therapy is a form of 3D-CRT radiation therapy. Just as in 3D-CRT, the prostate is treated with photon radiation from multiple angles every day. Yet the IMRT beam strength (intensity) can be modified (modulated) in every beam. In other words, a portion of the beam can be stronger in one area and weaker just fractions of a centimeter away. It would be like putting a filter in front of a single flashlight beam, making half of it faint while the rest of the beam remains at full intensity.

The radiation beams are shaped and modulated using a computerized device known as a multileaf collimator (MLC), which is positioned at the point where radiation exits the linear accelerator. The MLC controls the shape, size, and timing of the beams. This allows even higher doses of radiation to be delivered to the prostate while maintaining low doses to the normal tissue.

Intensity modulated radiation therapy is proving to be an excellent way of delivering radiation to the prostate while decreasing the rate of side effects associated with the other types of external beam radiation. At Memorial Sloan-Kettering Cancer Center, a study of 772 prostate cancer patients who received IMRT between 1996 and 2001 showed a significant decline in the number of men who experienced rectal problems compared to what's been seen with 3D-CRT.[12] Also, the short-term PSA control rate appeared to be about equal to the results of 3D-CRT radiation. Thus, IMRT seems to provide PSA control rates similar to 3D-CRT with fewer immediate and long-term effects to the rectum.

In His Words

George Harding didn't think that prostate cancer would ever enter his life. But a prostate specific antigen (PSA) test in 1995 brought that idea crashing down. After consulting with different doctors, he was presented with the idea of undergoing 3D-CRT—a treatment his primary care physician fully supported.

"After being diagnosed, I thought I was going to die the next day because I didn't fully understand prostate cancer at the time. But once I figured out I wasn't going to die, I adjusted pretty quickly.

"I was not too sure about having surgery because just six months before I was diagnosed, my wife's cousin, who was in his 60s, died as the surgeon was trying to remove his cancerous prostate.

"I went to another urologist for an opinion. This doctor's rule of thumb was that if you're in your 50s, it's surgery. When you're in your 60s, it's a toss-up between the surgery, radiation, or other treatments. When you're in your 70s, like I was, he said it was radiation or a treatment other than surgery.

"When I was at this urologist's office, a representative came in and asked if I wanted to participate in a program looking at 3D-CRT. I later talked with my primary doctor about it, and he said, 'Go for it.'

"I went every day for 42 days except Saturdays and Sundays. The treatment itself was just like lying on a table and going to sleep. I had no immediate side effects at all—no bowel or urination problems.

"Now my PSA is at 0.55, and it's been there for some time. As far as long-lasting side effects, I can't get an erection. It took a couple of years before I couldn't have any erections. I can't take Viagra because I have heart disease. But, not having erections is not a big deal. I have a great wife. We've been married for 62 years. And you don't have to have sex in order to have love. You can love a person without that.

"I didn't go to a support group. I preferred to handle this on my own. I did talk to my wife about it at the beginning. But, all in all, I never let the cancer worry me. I would say that if a person went into the treatment knowing that he is going to be cured, his attitude will help his recovery. No matter what happens, a positive attitude is going to help him a lot."

What is proton beam radiation?

Proton radiation is particle radiation. Unlike photon radiation—which is a wave that gives up most of its energy as it enters the body and whose strength decreases approximately evenly as it travels through tissues—proton beam radiation deposits its energy only as the particles begin to slow down. The distance that a proton of a given energy travels in human tissue before it slows down is well-known. So, by positioning the beam depth to deposit its energy only in the cancerous tissue, doctors hope to avoid many side effects often associated with radiation therapy. Proton radiation is ideal for cancers that require exceptionally delicate treatment, such as a tumor that wraps around the spinal cord or the optic nerve.

Radiation oncologists rarely use proton therapy as a sole treatment for prostate cancer. In those men who do receive it, it's most often combined with standard or conformal external beam radiation. The patients usually receive five weeks of standard or 3D-CRT radiation to the prostate, seminal vesicles, and possibly the lymph nodes, followed by two to three weeks of proton beam radiation to the prostate only.

There is some controversy regarding the value of proton therapy for prostate cancer, particularly since the equipment cost is typically more than 10 times greater than conventional 3D-CRT and IMRT-based photon therapy from a linear accelerator.

When a patient asks if he should get proton radiation for his prostate cancer, our best advice is that right now there's no proof that it works better in treating prostate cancer than current 3D-CRT and IMRT therapies. Nonetheless, it is expected that more results of proton therapy will be available in the coming years and better comparisons with linear accelerator-based treatments can be made.

What about neutrons?

Neutron beam radiation therapy relies on subatomic particles—neutrons—to defeat cancer cells. Neutron therapy has been associated with a greater degree of side effects to tissues around the prostate. A few U.S. centers are investigating it as a treatment. Similar to the situation with proton therapy, more results are needed to make appropriate comparisons.

In His Words

Prior to relocating to California with his partner, Terry Allen got a head-to-toe physical. His doctor said a PSA test was unnecessary because he was only 42, nor did his former physician give him a digital rectal exam (DRE). Only a few months later, Mr. Allen learned prostate cancer doesn't always wait until a man is over the age of 50.

"When I went in for a checkup, the doctor found a tumor that took up most of the prostate. He sent me to a urologist right away for a PSA. The PSA came back at 29. The six-core biopsy was positive. I slid into emotional and psychological numbness. As a gay man, seeing HIV around me was one thing; I had already dealt with others' deaths. I'm HIV negative, yet at 42 I was face-to-face with the prospect of my own death from cancer.

"Before totally ruling out surgery, I underwent a lymph node dissection, which was negative. Based on that information I chose IMRT. Before radiation, I had an MRI, which suggested involvement of the right seminal vesicle and the right vascular bundle. So, the IMRT radiation was conformed to take in those areas.

"I had 40 treatments. In the middle of it, I think that I had more frequent urination. I also had one episode of bleeding from the rectum. None of my physicians could determine if the bleeding was associated with the radiation. The bleeding interrupted treatment for a number of days, but it's never come back.

"I was also on hormones for a few months before treatment, during radiation, then for about 18 months afterward. Frankly, it was awful. Hot flashes were constantly present. I also lost my libido. I got depressed, too. I think it was as a result of all the hormonal suppression.

"Even though my partner was with me every step of the way, having cancer led me to examine a lot of my life, including my 19-year relationship. He and I separated for a time, but we got back together and now have an even better relationship.

"I've had no lasting bowel problems. I still urinate frequently, probably more than most men. Once I was off the hormones, my libido came back. My PSA leveled off at 0.7. It's been stable for over a year and a half.

"I am a proponent of radiation. I know there are a lot of complexities about treatment choices, but as a result of my experience, I encourage people to look at radiotherapy options. Think carefully and make decisions based on fact, not impulse."

How do doctors know where to target the radiation?

While the techniques of delivering conventional, 3D-CRT, and IMRT treatments are slightly different, the way doctors plan the treatment is generally similar. Planning begins with a CT scan of the prostate, from which the radiation oncologist outlines the treatment area.

Next, a team of radiation physicists and dosimetrists (the medical personnel who specialize in planning radiation doses) design the treatment field.

The target area conforms to the curve and shape of the patient's prostate. A small area around the prostate, including some of the bladder and the rectum, also receives radiation but it's mostly of a lower dose compared to what the prostate receives. This margin is by design because prostate cancer frequently spreads microscopically outside of the prostate and into the surrounding tissue. Such microscopic spread cannot be seen on diagnostic scans such as CTs or MRIs. The treatment margin ensures that the entire prostate is treated at every session. After the plan is completed, it's submitted to the radiation oncologist for review and approval.

Positioning is crucial in all types of external beam radiation. To make sure the photon radiation is right on target, the patient receives small, semipermanent marks on his skin. Before each day's session, the patient lies on the table and the technologists line up those marks to alignment lasers. These lasers are not at all harmful and are simply a means to make sure the patient is right where he needs to be for treatment.

I've heard that movement of the prostate can compromise external beam treatment, particularly the precise treatments such as IMRT and 3D-CRT. Can doctors do anything about this?

There are a number of studies showing that each day the prostate can be in a slightly different internal position. This may be due to the fullness of the bladder and rectum as well as the patient's position on the treatment table.

The treatment is designed to compensate for this prostate movement by treating a margin around the gland (discussed in the preceding answer). Another method to ensure the correct area is treated is to use daily ultrasound localization of the prostate. This means that when the patient is on the treatment table, a special ultrasound machine is used to determine the prostate position on that particular day. This isn't a foolproof method and although a number of centers are doing it, it's still being investigated to determine just how effective it is.

Another way of checking the prostate position calls for placing small metallic markers in the prostate prior to radiation therapy. A daily x-ray determines the positions of these markers, and the treatment team makes sure these markers fall within that day's radiation treatment. This method has not been widely adopted yet because it's still being studied, but it is showing great promise.

Finally, physicists and researchers from linear accelerator manufacturers and elsewhere are looking into ways that these machines can use the linear accelerators to show the position of the prostate and other organs adjacent to the prostate on a daily basis as the patient lies on the treatment table. It's hoped that this will be a reliable method of compensating for prostate movement and give doctors a better ability to deliver radiation at higher doses and with smaller margins. It is anticipated that such approaches will allow even higher doses of radiation to be delivered to the prostate and thus result in higher cure rates with fewer side effects.

How do doctors decide which radiation treatment is best for me?

The choice for therapy doesn't completely depend on the doctor's recommendation. You, the patient, play an important role in making this decision, too. For instance, some men who are candidates for radioactive seed therapy don't want permanent seeds and instead opt for external beam radiation. What the patient's insurance plan will cover, too, can be a factor.

Other dynamics influencing the kind of external beam therapy your doctor may recommend is what's available at the radiation center where he or she practices and the goal of the therapy. (The goal of therapy would be whether the doctors want to treat the prostate only, prostate plus seminal vesicles, or the pelvis. The therapeutic goal also takes into account the desired dose—lower dose for small cancers, higher for large cancers—and whether brachytherapy will be part of the overall treatment.)

Important Considerations for External Beam Radiation Therapy

What are the advantages of external beam radiation therapy?

With this therapy, patients avoid the risks commonly associated with surgery—adverse reaction to anesthesia, the potential for having to undergo a transfusion, and the time needed to recover from a surgical wound. Generally, no pain is associated with radiation therapy. Another benefit is that the immediate side effects are mild and generally do not limit day-to-day activities. Unlike surgery, the risk of urinary incontinence is very low, and external beam radiation is associated with fewer temporary initial urinary symptoms than seed implantation.

What are the disadvantages?

It's inconvenient. A full course of treatment requires eight weeks or more of daily visits to a cancer treatment center, five days per week for about 15 to 35 minutes each day. The rectum and colon are the most susceptible organs to be damaged from external beam radiation; between 5 percent and 15 percent of patients develop rectal problems.

Another potential—and controversial—disadvantage to external beam therapy is the radiation dose itself. The effective radiation dose delivered to the prostate via external beam is less than it is with radioactive seed implants. Retrospective studies in which patients are biopsied several years after receiving any form of radiation therapy tend to show residual or recurrent prostate cancer more frequently in patients who had external beam radiation than in patients with seed implants. It's important to note, however, that while there may be a higher incidence of recurrence with external beam, these retrospective studies *do not* necessarily show that there's a greater risk of developing a life-threatening recurrence. Therefore, without direct head-to-head clinical trials it is difficult to state with certainty whether there is any difference between external beam radiation therapy and seeds when it comes to curing prostate cancer. For most men diagnosed with early stage prostate cancer, when each treatment is done appropriately and with modern techniques, each offers a very high cure rate with a very low chance of dying from prostate cancer within 10 to 12 years of treatment.

What would make me a good candidate for external beam therapy?

Good candidates for surgery or seed implantation are also usually good candidates for external beam radiation. Also, good candidates are patients with an aversion to any kind of invasive procedure, patients who are too old for surgery, and men who are not good candidates for seed implants because of urinary difficulties due to benign prostatic hyperplasia (BPH).

What factors indicate that I should avoid external beam therapy?

Of all the treatments for prostate cancer that's confined to the gland—surgery, seed implantation, or external beam radiation—external beam is applicable to the largest range of patients. This is because the treatment is noninvasive and does not involve anesthesia or surgical time. Thus, patients who are in relatively poor health can easily tolerate this form of therapy. However, patients who have preexisting conditions of the rectum or colon, such as inflammatory bowel disease, are not good candidates for external beam therapy.

Patients who have a history of multiple abdominal surgeries often have considerable scar tissue within their abdomens, which may make the colon and intestines more susceptible to external beam radiotherapy damage, particularly if pelvic radiotherapy is given.

If patients have received any prior radiation therapy to the pelvic region for other cancers, further radiation usually cannot be used—but each case should be evaluated by a qualified radiation oncologist to establish this with certainty.

Can external beam therapy be used for aggressive, high-grade prostate cancer?

Unfortunately, high-grade cancers are not as likely as low-grade cancers to be cured with any single treatment method. For that reason, there is ongoing research to determine which local treatment or combination of treatments—such as radiation or surgery combined with hormone therapy or chemotherapy—are best.

External beam radiation alone, however, can cure 15 percent to 30 percent of men who have high-grade prostate cancer. More recent results from large clinical trials demonstrate that the combination of hormonal therapy with radiation offers better cure rates than older conventional radiation therapy alone.

I'm 58 years old. I know studies don't have long enough follow-up to show one treatment has a better 10-year survival or distant metastatic free survival than another. But I hope to live another 20 years. If I want a treatment that has the best chance of getting rid of all evidence of the disease, which should I receive?

One of the problems we have (fortunately) in comparing the effectiveness of prostate cancer treatments is the fact that most men diagnosed and treated for prostate cancer live 10 years or more, regardless of the treatment.

When someone states that "treatment A is more effective than treatment B," it's important to know what is being measured because there are quite a few different definitions of successful treatment.

If *overall survival* is what's being measured, there is no reasonable study that shows any difference in overall survival by treatment. If the measure is *distant metastatic disease free survival*, again, there is no significant survival difference among the various treatments for men with early stage, low-, or intermediate-risk disease.

However, if the measure is *biochemical relapse free survival* (BRFS)—meaning the PSA doesn't rise for two or three consecutive PSA tests—studies will show that different treatments do have different outcomes. But this seemingly clear statement comes with a catch. Comparing these BRFS studies is difficult because these studies don't define BRFS exactly the same way, and patients in each study are selected using different criteria. With that caveat, though, we can say that for low-risk and intermediate-risk patients, the best reported BRFS rates are from surgery or seed implants. Even 3D-CRT external beam radiation has not yet matched the 10-year BRFS rate reported by the top brachytherapy and surgical centers. Yet, because of the factors cited above, this subject is highly controversial and a matter of hot debate among prostate cancer experts. Even the most well-read experts could review the same studies and honestly come away with different conclusions.

I have existing erectile difficulties and some urinary problems. Will my doctor recommend external beam therapy?

Patients who have existing erectile difficulties will have a greater chance of erectile dysfunction following any treatment, including external beam. So, there is no particular reason to favor external beam therapy in patients who have existing erectile difficulties. Some physicians feel that patients who have a lot of urinary problems usually associated with BPH in addition to their prostate cancer might be better off with external beam radiation rather than seed implantation. This is because external beam radiation tends to be a bit gentler on the prostate than seed implantation.

But for those younger patients who have prostate cancer along with BPH that's causing a lot of urinary symptoms, we might recommend surgery because it would address both problems.

Will a previous transurethral resection of the prostate (TURP) prevent me from having external beam therapy?

With a TURP, a portion of the prostate around the urethra is removed to improve urinary flow. This operation causes scar tissue to form and leaves a small cavity in the upper part of the prostate. Some doctors feel that the slight damage caused by the TURP operation can increase the risk of bleeding or incontinence following radiation treatments. Since external beam radiation is the most "gentle" form of radiation therapy for the prostate, it may be the preferred method of treatment for patients who have had a previous TURP.

The Most Common Side Effects

What are the immediate side effects of external beam radiation therapy?

Prostate cancer patients have few, if any, side effects during the first weeks of external beam radiation. As time goes on, though, they're likely to begin experiencing bowel and bladder symptoms. A significant portion of patients develop urinary urgency and frequency after a few weeks of treatment. Many patients also report some rectal urgency and increased frequency of bowel movements. Patients may experience temporary rectal irritation that could result in more frequent bowel movements, a bit of soreness in the anal area, or diarrhea. These symptoms usually resolve in a matter of a few weeks or a few months, but a small proportion of patients may be left with some permanent bowel problems.

For patients with high-grade, more aggressive disease, it is often common to apply radiation to the pelvic lymph nodes in case the disease has spread. Because of the location of the pelvic lymph nodes, it's impossible to avoid including some of the intestines in the radiation field. That's why patients who have their pelvic nodes treated are more likely to experience more frequent bowel movements and perhaps diarrhea. These symptoms are usually temporary and sometimes we suggest using medication to help with these transient symptoms if they are bothersome.

Nausea that's associated with radiation for prostate cancer is uncommon. Some patients experience a minor loss of pubic hair, although this is uncommon. Significant fatigue attributed to radiation treatment for prostate cancer doesn't happen very often, but mild fatigue may occur. This usually goes away a few weeks after treatment ends.

Is radiation therapy painful?

Radiation therapy, by itself, does not directly cause pain. However, it can irritate sensitive tissues such as the cells lining the rectum or hemorrhoidal tissue, which can lead to temporary rectal pain. If this symptom occurs, it's often treated with suppositories containing cortisone. Also, radiation can irritate the lining of the bladder or urethra to create some discomfort with urination. When this happens, over-the-counter pain medication may help, but many patients get by without any treatment because the irritation is usually mild and goes away within a few days to a few weeks after treatment.

Do I have to give up any of my regular physical activities during treatment?

We recommend that you maintain your normal lifestyle during treatment. However, if you like vigorous exercise, you may find yourself with less energy and a lower ability to push yourself to your physical limit. In this case, we urge you to listen to your body and be prepared to cut back on the intensity of exercise if you feel fatigued.

Will I be able to continue to have sex during the course of radiation?
Yes. Having sex is not only possible and safe but encouraged in order to maintain erection ability. Radiation treatments do not make the semen radioactive, so there is no danger to your partner.

While sexual activity during the course of radiation is possible and encouraged, it may be somewhat problematic. It is not uncommon for patients to have more difficulty achieving erections during radiation treatment because of the expected irritation around the prostate. Some men will experience a few minutes of mild to moderate burning associated with orgasm. This is not harmful but it may be disconcerting if they don't know this burning might occur. Nonsteroidal medication such as Aleve or ibuprofen, taken an hour or two before sex, can help decrease or prevent this burning sensation.

Psychological factors may come into play as well. Men may lose their sex drive not because of physical factors, but because the anxiety of undergoing cancer treatment weighs on their minds to the point of diminishing libido.

Are there long-term effects from conventional radiation? And what about long-term side effects from 3D-CRT and IMRT?
The rectum and bowel are the primary areas of concern following external beam treatments. In general, the older and simpler the radiation approach, the greater the chances of permanent bowel complications. The newer forms of 3D-CRT and IMRT treatments are less likely to leave the patient with long-term bowel difficulties, but there is always some risk.

Long-term rectal problems such as rectal bleeding (radiation proctitis) or a tendency for diarrhea have been reported in as many as 20 percent of patients or as few as 3 percent of patients, depending on the medical study and the degree of sophistication of external beam delivery. That being said, most radiation physicians would predict that somewhere between 5 percent and 10 percent of patients experience some bowel problem following conventional external beam radiation. The severity of these side effects is often mild. Radiation proctitis can happen anywhere from six months to several years following treatment. Radiation proctitis may be evident only by small amounts of blood on the tissue paper following a bowel movement. Often this bleeding is so minor that it does not affect a patient's blood count or require any therapy, and it usually goes away on its own. If radiation proctitis needs to be treated, it is best treated conservatively with suppositories, creams, and diet control. Typically, less than one out of 500 patients has rectal damage needing surgical repair.

We have a word of caution for those patients who do develop radiation proctitis. If a biopsy is taken from the area of radiation proctitis, that biopsy often aggravates the condition. Many gastroenterologists don't know this. So, if you begin to experience a small amount of rectal bleeding months after radiation therapy for prostate cancer and another physician recommends a biopsy, be sure to talk with your radiation oncologist first.

Another long-term problem that can occur has to do with urination. If an external beam patient is going to develop a long-term urinary side effect, it will more likely be urinary frequency and urgency (meaning patients need to get up more at night to urinate, and it's difficult to wait for very long to relieve oneself) rather than leaking urine.

If the bladder is damaged by radiation, blood in the urine can be seen. Similar to rectal bleeding, this side effect also happens months to years later and it recurs frequently. Occasionally, bleeding has to be controlled by an endoscopic procedure or medication. On rare occasions, the radiation can result in scarring of the urethra and lower bladder regions so that a narrowing of the urinary channel occurs, which may require surgery to open up the areas, but this only occurs in a very small percentage of men.

Erectile dysfunction (ED) is a common problem following external beam radiation. Its time of onset is a little longer than what occurs after surgery because it takes some time for the radiation to affect the vessels feeding blood to the erection mechanism. It is not uncommon for the onset of ED to occur six months to several years following external beam radiation. Since it's rare that radiation therapy does complete damage to the nerves in charge of erections, radiation patients often respond to medication, such as Viagra, better than patients who had surgery.

Will my age play a part in whether or not I'll experience sexual dysfunction or incontinence after external radiation?

In most studies of erectile dysfunction following surgery, seed implantation, or external beam radiation, age has been found to be a contributing factor in the occurrence of ED. As men age, it is common for erection ability to decline, become weaker, and, therefore, be more likely to be damaged by any treatment including external beam radiation, although this has not been studied thoroughly.

If patients have other medical problems, such as diabetes or cardiovascular disease, most studies indicate that they, too, will be more susceptible to ED following any treatment. So, it would appear that the patient's level of sexual functioning prior to therapy is probably more important than his exact age.

The development of incontinence following external beam radiation is not related specifically to the patient's age. Incontinence is more common in patients who have had prior surgery, such as a TURP, or who have some weakness of their pelvic musculature, leading to difficulty with urination control. These factors are more related to a man's general health than they are to his specific age, but typically the risk of developing any urinary incontinence following external radiation therapy is less than 1 percent.

If I'm fully potent prior to external beam radiation, how are my chances of retaining potency afterward?

Sexual potency in men can be influenced by a number of factors including age, medication use, tobacco use, and overall health (including cardiovascular problems, diabetes, and hypertension). Because so many factors affect potency, it is difficult to measure the precise effect that radiation therapy may have on a man's sexual potency. Current figures indicate that 10 percent to 50 percent of men may develop some degree of erectile dysfunction following radiation therapy, which may be temporary or long lasting. Nevertheless, some studies show there is good news for men with good sexual function prior to radiation therapy who develop some limitations afterward. Viagra can help 80 percent to 90 percent of them maintain sexual function.

What kind of follow-up will I have after radiation to know if it is killing the cancer?

Follow-up after radiation treatment is not significantly different than follow-up after surgery. In both instances, PSA measurements are the cornerstone of the checkups. However, the PSA response following either radiation or seeds acts somewhat differently than it does after surgery. Surgery should completely remove the prostate and the prostate cancer. Therefore, the PSA is expected to drop to very low levels, usually undetectable, within three weeks of the surgery. But after radiation, the prostate gland can produce some PSA as the radiation is destroying cancerous and normal prostate cells. This time frame seems to be variable in different patients, and, therefore, the PSA decline after radiation can vary considerably from patient to patient.

Postradiation follow-up usually consists of obtaining a PSA level every three to six months for the first several years. If an individual's PSA drops very quickly to extremely low levels (0.5 ng/mL) and stays there for several consecutive measurements, then the follow-ups are usually increased to every 6 to 12 months between measurements. If, on the other hand, the PSA is fluctuating or going down very slowly, additional PSA tests may remain at three months or may occur more frequently. Usually no other follow-up testing (bone scans, CT scans, MRIs, or another biopsy of the prostate) is done unless the PSA shows a significant rise after radiation treatment.

For those who experience unusual or excessive side effects, the follow-up may be different. Such follow-up might entail examination of the rectum and colon for bleeding problems or examinations of the bladder or urethra for urinary problems.

If I still have a measurable PSA after treatment, does this mean that cancer cells are still in my prostate?

No. Normal prostate cells and cancerous prostate cells both produce PSA. Because of their long cell cycle time, it takes a while for both the cancer and normal cells to die, so PSA may be still be produced for some years. Also, there may be some residual normal cells remaining that result in PSA being detected in the blood.

We would like to emphasize that several years after treatment with either seed implantation or external beam radiation, a patient's PSA is expected to be stable with very little fluctuation. The PSA does not necessarily have to be zero to indicate successful treatment. Again, this is because there may be some normal cells remaining, particularly after external beam radiation. These cells can produce a little bit of PSA. So, it is the *stability* of the PSA that is the most important feature. Most patients get to a PSA that's below 1.0 ng/mL, but many achieve PSAs lower than 0.5 ng/mL, and some below 0.2 ng/mL.

A final word about external beam radiation. Although complications can and do occur, the vast majority of patients tolerate external beam radiation quite well. It's been a standard of therapy for prostate cancer for decades, and new ways of delivering it are only making it better.

8

Brachytherapy for Prostate Cancer: Are Seeds the Way to Go?

Daniel H. Clarke, M.D.; Brian J. Moran, M.D.;
Anthony L. Zietman, M.D.; John C. Blasko, M.D.

THE IDEA TO implant radioactive sources inside the body to eradicate cancer is at least a century old. In July 1903 Alexander Graham Bell—yes, the one who invented the telephone—wrote to a physician who was experimenting with radium treatments, "There is no reason why a tiny fragment of radium sealed up in a fine glass tube should not be inserted into the very heart of the cancer, thus acting directly upon the diseased material. Would it not be worthwhile making experiments along this line?"

The first use of internal radiation to fight prostate cancer came just a few years later. Two physicians put a small amount of radium in a tube, placed that tube into a catheter, pushed it into the prostatic urethra, and left it in place for several hours. Patients usually required several treatments over many weeks. Uncomfortable, yes, but the doctors reported some success.

Different doctors tried a variety of things during the next several decades in hopes of improving internal radiation. The most significant breakthrough came in the 1970s when physicians in New York surgically implanted radioactive iodine-125 seeds. They loaded the seeds into long, hollow needles; surgically opened the abdomen; and injected the seeds into the prostate. The problem was that the seeds were often poorly distributed—some spots received too much radiation, while other areas received too little.

It wasn't until the 1980s that Dr. Hans Holm at the University of Copenhagen figured out how to evenly distribute the seeds without performing open surgery. After giving a patient an epidural anesthesia, Dr. Holm inserted an ultrasound probe into the rectum. The sound waves transmitted a clear on-screen image. This allowed Dr. Holm and his team to watch what they were doing as they put the seed-bearing needles through the perineum and into the prostate.

The modern prostate brachytherapy procedure has continued to evolve and improve. The first transrectal ultrasound and template-guided prostate brachytherapy procedure was performed in Seattle, Washington, by Drs. John Blasko and Haakon Ragde in 1985. Today the procedure is successfully performed in hundreds of centers throughout the world.

The procedure is usually thought of as a three-part process. The first is the planning phase, in which the patient's prostate is carefully measured by ultrasonography. That information is then subjected to computer analysis to determine the appropriate number of seeds, seed strength (measured in millicuries), and the geometry of seed arrangement within the prostate. This planning process may be done a few weeks prior to the procedure or it may be performed in the operating room in conjunction with the actual seed insertion.

The second part of the procedure is the seed insertion into the prostate. This requires an anesthetic of some type and is usually performed in either a hospital operating room or an outpatient surgery center. Needles are inserted through the skin between the legs (the perineum) and into the prostate under the guidance of real-time imaging from an ultrasound probe, which has been placed into the patient's rectum. A customized plan is made for each patient. The number, strength, and location of seeds depend upon the shape and size of the patient's prostate and the dose prescribed by the radiation oncologist.

Most of the time patients do not need to remain overnight in the hospital and can go home immediately following the implant. It is this convenience of treatment and rapid return to everyday activities that make seed implants very appealing. The final step after the implant procedure is a CT scan of the prostate and the seeds to determine that all the seeds are in proper position. This scan occurs anywhere from a day to a month after the patient goes home.

In this chapter, we take a close look at today's sophisticated treatment, patients who are the best candidates, and what patients can expect immediately after the procedure.

Brachytherapy Basics

What is brachytherapy?

Prostate seed implantation is a form of radiation treatment in which radioactive materials are placed directly into a cancer-affected organ with the intent of destroying the malignancy. Brachytherapy may be thought of as internal radiation.

The technical term for prostate permanent seed implantation is *prostate brachytherapy* (brāke-therapy). *Brachy* is a Greek prefix meaning "short." So, *brachytherapy* literally means therapy that comes from a short distance away. The prostate receives a high dose of radiation to fight cancer while the bladder, rectum, and bowel receive very little radiation.

What are the advantages of prostate brachytherapy?

The most important advantage is that the cure rates are excellent. No other type of radiation is capable of delivering a higher dose to the prostate, which is reassuring for getting rid of the cancer. In terms of convenience, it's a one-time, minimally invasive procedure that requires less than one hour of spinal, epidural, or general anesthesia. Recovery times are short and patients can generally return to their normal routines within a few days. Although temporary urinary side effects are expected for a few months, the vast majority of patients have no long-term problems with urination or bowel function.

Is brachytherapy a successful treatment?

The modern method of prostate brachytherapy is yielding excellent results in controlling cancer, as evidenced by a 2001 study published in the *International Journal of Radiation, Oncology, Biology, Physics*. This clinical investigation, led by the doctors at Seattle Prostate Institute, showed that 87 percent of 125 patients with early stage cancer (prostate specific antigen [PSA] less than 10 ng/mL, Gleason score 2–6, T1–T2b) who received iodine-125 seeds as their sole form of treatment showed no evidence of disease at 10 years. (See Table 8.1.) What's more, the vast majority of patients achieved a PSA of 0.2 ng/mL. According to the study, with seed implants, a patient's PSA usually declines to 0.2 ng/mL or less. Thus this study revealed that with seed implants a high percentage of patients can expect to be cured 10 years or more after treatment. However, it may take seven or eight years for the PSA to reach 0.2 ng/mL or lower.

As far as actual cancer recurrence, only 3 percent of patients had cancer recur in the prostate and another 3 percent had prostate cancer recur in another part of the body. The remaining 4 percent who were considered failures only had rises in PSA—no actual cancer could be discovered by testing. At the time of publication, no patients in this study who received prostate brachytherapy had died of prostate cancer.

There is one other intriguing aspect to this study. This group of men, who were all treated between 1988 and 1990, had a much higher rate of progression-free survival compared to a similar group of patients treated in 1986 and 1987. The conclusion is that physicians greatly improved their brachytherapy techniques after 1987, which has resulted in even better long-term, progression-free survival. It is probable that further refinements in technique that have been adopted since this study means that today's outcomes are likely to be even better.

TABLE 8.1   Five- and 10-Year Biochemical Relapse-Free Survival

Urologists and radiation oncologists evaluate the effectiveness of prostate cancer treatment by following PSA levels in patients. If the PSA level falls to a low level and stays low after treatment, the patient is biochemically free of disease (BRFS stands for biochemical relapse-free survival).

This table compares the 5- and 10-year rates of BRFS reported in various studies. Note that comparing the effectiveness of one treatment to another is difficult for reasons that include: differing definitions of BRFS, bias in patient selection from one center to the next (for instance, one center has more favorable patients than another center), different definitions of "risk group" (especially intermediate risk group), differences in how long patients were followed, use of hormone therapy (which can affect the PSA reading), and, most important, the lack of any modern randomized trial comparing one treatment to another.

Still, we do need to make comparisons to reach any kind of decision. Dividing patients into "risk groups" (based on biopsy Gleason score, PSA, and rectal exam findings) helps to even out the differences in patient selection from one center to another, somewhat. But even with this, there are different definitions in risk group that lead to different results as shown in the 10-year BRFS data from Sylvester et al. (these 232 patients all received seeds and external beam radiation in Seattle, but the results vary with the various risk group definitions).

| | 5-YEAR BRFS | | | | | 10-YEAR BRFS | | |
| | Surgery D'Amico[1] | 3D-CRT Zelefsky[2] | Pd¹⁰³ Seeds Blasko[3] | I¹²⁵ Seeds Grimm[4] | | I¹²⁵/Pd¹⁰³ Seeds + ebrt Sylvester[5] | | |
Risk Group	(HUP) DRG	(B&W) DRG	(MSKCC) SRG	(Seattle) SRG	(Seattle) SRG	(Seattle) SRG	(Seattle) MRG	(Seattle) DRG
Low	85%	83%	90%	94%	87%	85%	84%	84%
Intermediate	65%	50%	70%	82%	76%	77%	93%	90%
High	32%	28%	47%	65%	—	47%	57%	46%

1. J Clin Oncol. 2000; 18:1164–1172.
2. J Urol. Vol. 166, pp 876–881, Sept. 2001 (≥75Gy) (39% underwent hormone tx).
3. Int. J Radiat Oncol Biol Phy. 2000; 46:839–850.
4. Int. J Radiat Oncol Biol Phy. 2001; 51:31–40.
5. Presented ASTRO 2002, submitted to IJROBP 2003.

HUP: Hospital University of Pennsylvania
B&W: Brigham and Women's Hospital
SRG: Simple Risk Group definition
MRG: Mount Sinai Medical Center Risk Group definition
DRG : D'Amico Risk Group definition

What are the disadvantages?

One of the main disadvantages of prostate brachytherapy is that most patients temporarily experience moderate to severe urinary urgency and frequency, and a weak urinary stream for several months, especially at night. These urinary side effects are more pronounced than what patients experience with external beam radiation. In addition, a small proportion of men

---

In His Words

Carson Pierce, a dentist, was diagnosed with prostate cancer at age 54. Instead of letting the shock and fear paralyze his decision-making ability, Dr. Pierce talked with friends in the medical field about what they would do. He also interviewed dozens of patients before making his decision.

"I was diagnosed with prostate cancer in 1995. Before I made any decision, my urologist asked me to read about my choices, which I did. I also called local urologists to see if I could talk with some of their patients. Over the course of a year, I talked with probably 30 surgical patients, each within a year of their surgeries. They told me they could have erections with the help of Viagra. Yet, they were wearing pads because of incontinence. There's only one man that I came across who had no erectile or incontinence problems after his nerve-sparing surgery.

"A friend talked to me about seed implants. I traveled to a center across the country to see if I was a candidate. I spent the day with the doctors there and did all the tests. Based on the results of their tests and the outcomes of the CT and bone scans done here in Atlanta, they said that I was a candidate for seeds.

"But I didn't stop my research. For the next few months, I talked to surgical patients, seed patients, and hormone patients. The more I learned, the more I knew that the seed implant was the way for me.

"The following June, my wife and I flew across the country so I could have the implant. I didn't have any post-op discomfort. I never took a pain pill. I have no long-term side effects—no bowel side effects, no urinary problems, and no erectile problems. I've had two biopsies over the past five years and there are no signs of cancer. I understand that I still might have prostate cancer cells in my body. They could have escaped before treatment. Even if I had had surgery, they could have gotten out. But I have peace of mind that my treatment worked. My goal and my objective was quality of life, and I attained that."

---

will find that they are unable to urinate at some stage over the first few weeks after the procedure. If this is the case, a catheter may be required. (A catheter is most unusual after external beam radiation.)

Another disadvantage of both prostate brachytherapy and external beam radiation is that there has not been an opportunity for surgical staging. Through an operation, more details of a patient's cancer status can be learned by testing the lymph nodes and performing a microscopic examination of the tissues surrounding the prostate. These additional tests can give a clearer picture of the extent of the patient's disease, supplementing the prognostic information gleaned from the patient's Gleason score and PSA. With today's early detection, cancer spread to the lymph nodes is rare.

Still one more disadvantage is that following prostate brachytherapy, the PSA sometimes takes many years to achieve a nadir (the lowest point). Achieving a nadir provides reassurance that the cancer is in remission. In addition, the PSA can fluctuate in the first two or three years due to the "PSA bounce" phenomenon. (PSA bounce is discussed in Chapter 9.) Patients must tolerate this uncertainty for several years following brachytherapy.

What kind of patient is best suited for seed therapy?

Most patients who are good candidates for radical prostatectomy are also candidates for seed therapy alone (called monotherapy, meaning no other form of treatment is used along with the seeds). However, the prostate gland must not be too large (it should be less than 60 grams or 60 cc). Ideally, the best candidates for seed monotherapy are patients with a PSA less than 10, Gleason score of 6 or less, and a DRE that does not suggest the tumor has extended outside the prostate. Because patients with significant urinary problems from benign prostatic hyperplasia (BPH) may have even more severe urinary problems after a seed implant, they may be better served with external beam radiation or radical prostatectomy.

Can I still be treated with seeds alone if my Gleason score is higher than 6 and PSA is greater than 10?

Possibly. A patient with intermediate- or high-risk disease may be a candidate for implant alone, but it's usually recommended that he get external beam radiation and seeds together. A PSA that's higher than 10 ng/mL but less than 20 ng/mL may be considered for an implant alone if there is only a small percentage of cancer in the biopsy cores, the doctor cannot feel any significant lumps or hardness during a DRE, and the Gleason score is less than 7. Some patients with a Gleason 7, a PSA less than 10 ng/mL, and only one or two positive biopsy cores can also be treated with seeds alone.

In His Words

Chad Casey is a youthful 71-year-old retired Seattle resident who is happily married. Over the years, Mr. Casey was adamant about getting annual exams. The only year he skipped was 1998 when his doctor retired. He found a new physician and when he went in for his 1999 annual exam, Mr. Casey figured he would be in and out of the office, just like all the years before.

"Finding the lump in my prostate took me by surprise. My doctor referred me to a urologist, who ordered a biopsy. Later, the urologist called and suggested that my wife and I come in because they found cancer.

"The urologist suggested how we could take care of this thing—surgery, or external beam, or seeds. I was opposed to surgery. I made an appointment with a brachytherapist. During the first appointment he suggested getting a seminal vesicle biopsy. I did that and the report came back benign. I went back to the brachytherapist and we decided on external beam and seeds.

"I had external beam treatment for five weeks. After the radiation, I was off for a couple of weeks before the implant. I had a little more bleeding than was normal after the implant, but I was otherwise fine.

"As far as side effects, five nights after the implant, I got up five times. A few weeks later, it was four times . . . then two times . . . then one time. It was about six weeks before I slept through the night.

"There were only two subsequent effects. The first was radiation proctitis. A couple of years after the implant, during a routine exam that included a DRE [digital rectal exam], I had a lot of bleeding from the rectum. But, I've had no bleeding problems since that first incident.

"The other thing is that my erections haven't been as strong. Sexual intercourse is not very good. I don't believe in taking pills, so I don't take Viagra. My PSA is now 0.1, and I feel as healthy as I did before treatment.

"Get all the information you can. But, you also have to trust the doctors in order to make a proper decision about what's best for your future. The second piece of advice is to go to a support group. These groups let you know you're not alone. Down the line, everyone begins to wonder, 'Did we get it all? Will it come back?' In a group, you find people who had the same type of treatment years before you did. And you see they're doing fine."

Is age a factor for selecting seeds?

Age is only a *relative* factor. There are 65-year-olds with serious conditions who are unlikely to live 10 years, and 75-year-olds in good health whose life span could be another decade or longer. Thus, while the average life expectancy of a 77-year-old man is 10 years, his overall health is more important than his age in choosing a specific treatment.

For very young men who have a life expectancy of more than 20 years, there may be a hesitation for recommending seed implants. This is because the available information for seed implants is currently at 10 to 15 years.

There is also a rare possibility that a patient might develop a different, radiation-induced cancer in the bladder or rectum. Radiation-induced cancers are extremely rare and take 15 to 30 years to develop, but this could be an issue for men in their 40s or early 50s.

I have existing urinary problems, but I'm otherwise in fine health. Am I a good candidate for implantation?

Whether existing urinary problems affect a patient's candidacy for implantation depends on the type and severity of urinary problems. As men age, most develop some symptoms of BPH but these symptoms would not be a hindrance to implantation as long as the symptoms are not severe. A common tool to evaluate the nature and severity of urinary symptoms is the American Urological Association Symptom Score Sheet (see Table 8.2).

There are no fixed rules regarding the use of this test but in general, if the patient's score is 10 or less he is less likely to have problems following seed implantation. If his score is between 10 and 19, he is usually still a candidate for seed implantation but may have to put up with a little more in the way of urinary symptoms during the first few months following his implant. Patients who score more than 19 points should understand that they may have more severe symptoms. It is still possible to do seed implants in these cases, but other factors, such as prostate size and response to urinary medicines, need to be considered. The determination of whether a patient is a candidate for prostate brachytherapy from the standpoint of their existing urinary status may require additional testing, such as a flow rate test, postvoid residual determination, and cystoscopy by a urologist who is experienced and knowledgeable in seed implants.

TABLE 8.2   AUA Symptom Score Sheet

Circle One Number on Each Line	Not at all	Less than 1 time in 5	Less than half the time	About half the time	More than half the time	Almost always
Over the past month or so, how often have you had a sensation of not emptying your bladder completely after you finished urinating?	0	1	2	3	4	5
During the past month or so, how often have you had to urinate again less than two hours after you finished urinating?	0	1	2	3	4	5
During the past month or so, how often have you stopped and started again several times when you urinated?	0	1	2	3	4	5
During the past month or so, how often have you found it difficult to postpone urination?	0	1	2	3	4	5
During the past month or so, how often have you had a weak urinary stream?	0	1	2	3	4	5
During the past month or so, how often have you had to push or strain to begin urination?	0	1	2	3	4	5

	None	1 time	2 times	3 times	4 times	5 or more
Over the past month, how many times per night did you most typically get up to urinate from the time you went to bed at night until the time you got up in the morning?	0	1	2	3	4	5

Add the score for each number above and write the total in the space to the right. Total: _____

Symptom Score: 1–7 (Mild)   8–19 (Moderate)   20–35 (Severe)

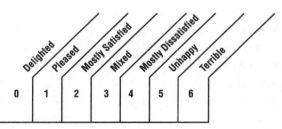

Quality of Life	Delighted	Pleased	Mostly Satisfied	Mixed	Mostly Dissatisfied	Unhappy	Terrible
How would you feel if you had to live with your urinary condition the way it is now, no better, no worse, for the rest of your life?	0	1	2	3	4	5	6

Can I be treated with seeds if the cancer is outside of the gland?

The question of cancer being outside of the gland can mean many different things. In the worst-case scenario, the cancer can spread from the prostate gland through the bloodstream to the bones. In this case, treatment of the prostate with seeds would not be appropriate.

Spread outside the gland could also mean spread through the lymphatic system to the lymph nodes in the pelvis or abdomen. Most patients with lymphatic spread cannot be cured. However, recent research suggests that some patients can be cured, but they would require a combination of several treatments and seeds might or might not be part of that plan.

Prostate cancer can also spread by direct local extension, whereby small fingers of cancer may grow through the capsule of the prostate and involve the surrounding fat, nerve bundles, or seminal vesicles. This extracapsular extension is divided into two groups: (1) focal or minimal and (2) extensive. Neither type of extracapsular extension can be accurately detected by CT scans, but the typical spread is only a couple of millimeters. This spread can be easily addressed by the seed implant since radiation implants are designed to reach outside the prostate an average of five millimeters or more. The profile of a patient's disease—the Gleason score, number of positive biopsies, and the PSA level—are taken into consideration to determine whether further testing is necessary to look for extensive extracapsular extension. An endorectal coil MRI with or without spectroscopy may assist in identifying these more extensive cancers. Sometimes these tests do not clearly show cancer spread, but there may be enough worry about spread that doctors will recommend different combinations of hormones, radiation, and brachytherapy to cover areas of the pelvic lymph nodes, seminal vesicles, or tissues surrounding the prostate in an effort to maximize the chances of cure.

If the seminal vesicles are positive for cancer, will they get implants or will the external beam radiation cover them?

The seminal vesicles lie above the prostate, behind the back wall of the bladder. Fortunately, the incidence of seminal vesicle involvement is low and falling year by year. The lowermost portions of the seminal vesicles always receive radiation from the seeds. But seeds alone cannot treat the entire seminal vesicles. If the whole seminal vesicle needs to be treated, then external beam radiation therapy must be added. If a biopsy of the seminal vesicles is positive or other scans such as CT or MRI show *unequivocally* that the seminal vesicles are cancerous, external beam radiation alone is generally selected in these cases.

Several institutions are treating patients with limited seminal vesicle involvement with hormones, external beam radiation, and seed implantation with seeding of the lower portion of the seminal vesicles.

I had a transurethral resection of the prostate (TURP) a few years ago. Can I get seeds?

The issue for a TURP patient really boils down to how much tissue was removed. TURPs done 15 to 20 years ago were often extensive, leaving only a small amount of prostate tissue. The early experience of seed implantation in TURP patients resulted in a high rate of incontinence, up to 35 percent. However, these early patients also received higher doses of radiation to the TURP defect than we would deliver with current brachytherapy techniques.

Today, TURP patients are treated with more seeds placed into the periphery of the gland and less in the center (this is called a peripheral loading pattern). This approach significantly lowers the dose to the TURP area, thereby reducing the risk of incontinence to 5 percent to 10 percent. Therefore, TURP patients can be successfully implanted if they have good urinary continence and the prostate volume study shows that a good deal of prostate tissue remains.

What is a pubic arch evaluation?

The prostate sits behind the pubic arch, which is the V shape created where the pubic bones meet. (See Figure 8.1.) The pubic arch study is simply a rectal ultrasound or a CT scan done to evaluate the size of the arch and its relationship to the prostate.

A narrow pubic arch can block the implant needles from properly entering the correct targets within the gland.

If the prostate gland is large, can anything decrease its size?

Yes—hormonal therapy. Prostates can shrink anywhere from 30 percent to 50 percent with three to six months of hormones. The larger the gland, the longer the need for pre-implant hormonal therapy. Most prostates will shrink sufficiently with hormones, unless the gland is massively enlarged (such as being much greater than 100 cc).

If I'm jittery before this ultrasound, can I ask for a sedative?

Being relaxed during the volume study and pubic arch evaluation is important because the images from this ultrasound must be accurate; they are needed to plan the number and position of the seeds. Usually a careful discussion and explanation by the person doing the ultrasound will calm the patient. A light sedative may be used to minimize the jitters, but the sedative can take hours to wear off and the patient will need someone to drive him home.

Do I need antibiotics or pain medication for a transrectal ultrasound?

There should be little or no pain from an ultrasound. Neither antibiotics nor pain medication is needed unless a urinary catheter is used. If so, we

---

FIGURE 8.1   Pubic Arch Interference

Ideally, the pubic arch does not interfere with accessing the prostate for a seed implant. But if the prostate enlarges and portions of it are behind the pubic arch (as indicated by the dotted lines), a few months of hormonal therapy can be used to shrink the prostate to a size suitable for implant.

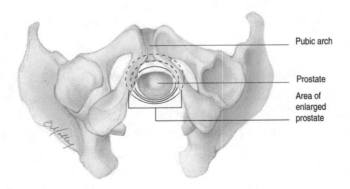

Pubic arch

Prostate

Area of enlarged prostate

---

may recommend a short course of antibiotics to prevent the possibility of urinary tract infection.

How do doctors "map" the prostate?

Mapping the prostate means using a series of images to outline the prostate. Mapping involves inserting the ultrasound probe into the rectum and then taking images of the prostate every five millimeters, from the base to the apex. This usually takes from 15 to 30 minutes.

What happens with the ultrasound images?

The radiation oncologist looks at each "slice" of the prostate and draws the area to be treated, which may include an extra margin of tissue in some areas around the gland. The radiation oncologist gives the physics team these images along with a prescription for how much radiation is needed. The physics team figures out where to place the seeds to create a cloud of radiation in and around the prostate gland while minimizing exposure to the bladder, urethra, and rectum. When the physics team is satisfied with this plan, they send it back to the radiation oncologist for final review and approval.

What is real-time dosimetry?

Most centers pre-plan the procedure several weeks before the implant. Some doctors, however, prefer to do the mapping and the physics work in the operating room. This is called real-time dosimetry or intra-operative planning. Although some doctors claim superiority of one method over another, there is no current evidence to indicate one planning method is better than another.

What's the difference between palladium-103 and iodine-125 seeds?

Both palladium and iodine give off very low-energy x-rays that only travel a short distance. This means that the dose of radiation delivered by both sources is confined to the prostate and the tissue immediately surrounding the gland.

The primary difference between the seeds is the rate at which the radiation is released. The palladium isotope gives up its energy faster than the iodine isotope. With palladium, the prostate receives the radiation dose much quicker so the side effects come on earlier than with iodine—and they may be slightly more intense. But they also tend to go away faster than iodine's side effects. The radiation from palladium does not travel quite as far as it does with iodine, which may result in a lower dose to surrounding organs, but it may also mean more cold spots within the implant if the implant is not done accurately (we explain cold spots a little later in this chapter). There is no evidence that one type of seed is more effective for cure than another.

Please explain seed half-life. How long will each kind of seed be radioactive?

Half-life is a physics term that means the time it takes for the isotope to release half of its radioactivity. The half-life for palladium-103 is 17 days. The half-life for iodine-125 is 60 days.

Generally, the seed implant is considered active for five half-lives. If the half-life for palladium-103 is 17 days, and it takes five half-lives for the seeds to release the bulk of their radiation, the seeds will be radioactive for 85 days. For an iodine-125 implant, the active life of the seeds is about 300 days.

Are the seeds permanent?

The physical seed is permanent but the radioactivity is not. The seeds are actually titanium tubes into which the radioactive material is placed. Titanium is used because the body does not reject it; titanium is the same material used for joint replacements, such as hips. Because the body does not treat titanium as a foreign substance, there is no danger from these inert seeds remaining in the body after the radiation disperses. Titanium is not magnetic, so if you have to have an MRI after a seed implant, it is perfectly safe to do so.

What is HDR?

HDR is the shorthand for high-dose rate brachytherapy. High-dose rate prostate brachytherapy is almost always combined with external beam radiation to treat early and locally advanced cancer. There is some experimental work using HDR alone, but the results are currently unknown.

The HDR procedure requires an inpatient hospital stay for a couple of days. Under ultrasound guidance and using a template similar to what's used in permanent seed implants, small catheters are placed through the perineum and into the prostate. Next, a computer-controlled device inserts a high activity iridium seed into each catheter. The treatment takes several minutes. Two or three treatments are given during a 24-hour period, and then the catheters are removed. No radioactive material remains in the prostate. Similar to seeds, this technology allows for the delivery of higher radiation doses than can be delivered with external beam radiation. However, the radiation from HDR is not higher than the doses from permanent seeds. Although the early results of HDR with external beam radiation are encouraging, this method of treating prostate cancer has not been as thoroughly studied as permanent seeds or external beam radiation.

In terms of treatment considerations, it's a little more difficult to undergo an HDR implant than a seed implant. This is because patients need to be in the hospital for two or three days with the needles and catheters in the prostate. But because radioactive material is removed from the prostate after only a few days, patients have a shorter duration of the temporary urinary side effects of frequency, urgency, and a slow urinary stream.

The Implant Procedure

What will happen when I check into the center? Will I be anesthetized for the implantation?

If you're like most patients, you'll spend between four to six hours at the hospital or surgical center from beginning to end. When you first check in, a preoperative nurse will give you a thorough reassessment, including asking about allergies, any current medications, and any unanswered questions you may have about the implant.

After signing the informed consent, you'll be taken to the operating room for anesthesia—general, epidural, or spinal. An epidural or spinal anesthesia blocks all sensation below the waist but patients may be given the option to remain fully awake and alert during the implant. Most men, though, prefer to have additional mild sedation. Patients who receive general anesthesia will be unconscious.

Who's in the operating room, and what are their roles?

In most centers, a radiation oncologist and an urologist perform the implant together. Each physician contributes specific skills to the procedure. Others in the operating room include operating room nurses, a nurse anesthetist and/or anesthesiologist, and someone from the physics team to track seed placement during the procedure and perform radiation surveys afterward. A radiation survey means taking measurements of the amount of emitted radiation from the seeds that were just placed. This is usually done by use of a Geiger counter placed for a few seconds at the surface of the patient's lower abdomen. The other purpose of a radiation survey is to check the used needles and bedding to be sure that no seed has inadvertently been left behind in the apparatus.

Who places the seeds into the needles?

A member of the physics team usually does this just before the procedure. There are a couple of different ways to get the seeds in the needles. Loose seeds can be loaded one by one into the needle until the correct number is in each needle. Companies that manufacture the seeds also make seeds held together with a suture material that the body absorbs. All that has to be done is count the number of needed seeds, cut, and drop that strand into the needle. Increasingly, manufacturers are able to provide needles that have already been loaded with seeds according to the physician's plan.

The loaded needles are inserted into holes in a radiation-shielded box that's identically coded with letters and numbers matching the template that's placed on the patient's perineum. The template identically matches the grid coordinates of the dosimetry plan that's derived from the ultrasound volume study.

How are the seeds placed?

After anesthesia, the nurses carefully place the patient into a modified lithotomy position, meaning the patient is on his back with his thighs at a 90-degree angle to his body, thighs apart, and lower legs placed in stirrups. The perineum is carefully cleaned with an antimicrobial agent and this area may be shaved depending on the practice of each center. The urethra is also identified. There are a couple of different ways of doing this. Some centers place a catheter into the urethra while others insert an aerated surgical jelly that shows up on the ultrasound.

The team assembles a stabilization system to support the implant equipment. The physician introduces an ultrasound probe into the rectum (which the patient won't feel due to the anesthesia), and then attaches that probe to the stabilization system. The final step is to attach a template grid to the stabilization system. This grid helps direct the needles through the perineum and into the correct locations within the prostate.

The doctor takes the needle from the needle box and inserts it into the corresponding template grid (see Figure 8.2). The doctor verifies the needle position and depth by looking at the ultrasound screen that has an identical grid image. The doctor also takes precise measurements to double-check the needle position prior to releasing seeds.

The entire procedure usually lasts from 30 minutes to two hours from the time the patient receives anesthesia until the implant is completed. Most implants require 16 to 30 needles and 60 to 130 seeds.

FIGURE 8.2   Placing the Seeds into the Prostate

After anesthesia, an ultrasound probe is placed in the rectum, a template grid is attached, and the needles are inserted through the perineum into the prostate. The needles are inserted through the grid holes as outlined in the radiation plan that was completed before the actual implant started.

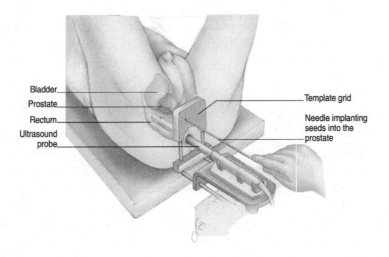

Bladder
Prostate
Rectum
Ultrasound probe
Template grid
Needle implanting seeds into the prostate

Is using a series of individual needles the only way to implant the seeds?

No. Another way to implant the seeds is via a cartridge system, usually known as a MICK applicator. In this system, specially designed empty needles are placed through the template and into the patient's prostate. When all of the needles are in the correct position, the MICK instrument is then attached to each of the needles in succession. The seeds have been loaded into cartridges, which are then fitted to the MICK instrument. By operating a plunger system, the seeds are deposited one at a time through the needle while another part of the apparatus retracts the needle at precise increments so that the seeds are accurately placed in the prostate from top to bottom.

Both the preloaded needle and cartridge technique are acceptable and reflect the training and preference of the physician.

Can I see what's going on during the procedure? Can I ask questions?

Patients who ask to remain awake after receiving spinal or epidural anesthesia will be able to hear what's going on. It's unlikely, however, that they will be able to see the actual implant. Doctors also encourage patients who remain awake to refrain from coughing, laughing, or boisterous conversation because these activities can be distracting or create unwanted movement of the prostate and/or misalignment of the template.

What is a cold spot?

Each seed releases radiation within a confined area, approximately the size of an eraser on the tip of a pencil. All of the seeds contribute some amount of radiation to the overall implant. However, if some seeds are too far apart, then the dose between the seeds may be inadequate to fight the cancer. This inadvertent underdosing is called a "cold spot." Skilled implant specialists will continually scan the length of the prostate with ultrasound during the procedure looking for areas devoid of seeds. If any develop, extra seeds are available to fill in these areas before the procedure is completed.

A "hot spot" is just the opposite. Seeds that are too close together create an area in which the radiation dose is too high. A small hot spot is unlikely to cause any side effects. But a large hot spot could injure the ure-thra, the urinary sphincter, or the rectum. Fortunately, sizeable hot spots are rare with today's preplanning methods.

Are the lymph nodes evaluated or treated during the procedure?

No. The vast majority of brachytherapy patients have a very low risk of lymph node involvement. If the lymph nodes were to be sampled, this would be done via an open operation or laparoscopically at a time other than dur-ing the brachytherapy procedure.

What is a cystoscopy?

We may look inside the patient's bladder at the end of the implant with an instrument called a cystoscope to make sure that no seeds strayed into the bladder. If there are blood clots or excessive bleeding, the bladder will be irrigated. The bladder will also be inspected to make sure there are no blad-der tumors. Some physicians avoid cystoscopies and instead use a catheter to flush out the bladder after the procedure in the event of blood clots or stray seeds. There is no preferred method.

Will I have any medication prior to the implant?

Most physicians prescribe antibiotics both before and after the implant. A few centers advocate the use of steroids prior to and for several days after the procedure to decrease swelling and prevent urinary blockage. Alterna-tively, some physicians use nonsteroidal anti-inflammatory medications such as ibuprofen or Aleve. Alpha-blocker medications (Flomax, Hytrin, or Car-dura) are very helpful in improving the strength of the urinary stream and are usually started before the procedure.

Immediately After the Implant

Will I experience pain and how long will it last?

There are two types of pain that patients may experience in the first day or two following seed implant. The first is an aching or tenderness between the legs where the needles were inserted. This is usually mild and only rarely requires pain medication. The second form of pain is a burning sensation when urinating. This pain is most severe the first several times the patient urinates following a seed implant. It then diminishes rapidly and usually does not last more than two or three days. Most patients are surprised at the lack of pain from this procedure; medicines such as Extra Strength Tylenol, Aleve, or ibuprofen are usually all that's needed. Occasionally a patient will take a stronger pain medication for a few days. Men may see a small amount of blood or small blood clots in their urine for a day or two. This is to be expected.

A few days later, a mild burning sensation may come back. It's uncommon and usually mild. It comes from the radiation doing its job of killing the cancer and decreases as the radiation wears off. It often lasts between three and six months, though a few patients report they've had this symptom for up to a year. In a few cases, the radiation may cause serious discomfort.

The best thing patients can do to minimize the burning is to drink plenty of water and take the prescribed medications. Water will dilute the urine to make it more comfortable as it passes through the urethra.

What Can I Do to Reduce Swelling?

Many doctors recommend using ice packs on the perineum off and on during the first 24 to 48 hours after the procedure. A great idea is to get three or four bags of frozen green peas and keep one on the perineum for 10 to 20 minutes. (You can also fill self-locking plastic bags with unpopped popcorn kernels and freeze.) Repeat this three to five times a day for the first two days after the implant. (Just be sure to throw out the peas or the popcorn kernels after you've finished with them as ice packs!)

An even better solution came from a patient's wife. Instead of using the whole bag of peas as a cold compress, she filled several surgical-like white latex gloves (readily available at most drugstores) with the frozen peas and tied off the tops. The glove's flexibility allowed her husband to easily and comfortably position this ingenious ice pack on his perineum. When one glove got warm, back into the freezer it went, simply to be replaced by another that was ready.

What happens if I find I can't empty my bladder at all?

The medical term for not being able to urinate is *acute urinary retention*. While a comparatively infrequent side effect after brachytherapy, it nevertheless happens in about 10 percent of cases. It occurs due to the radiation's irritating effects on the urethra and prostate and resultant swelling of the prostate. We treat it by inserting a catheter for a few days or even a few weeks. After a week of having a catheter in place, a "voiding trial" will be performed to see if the catheter is still needed. On rare occasions, a catheter may be necessary for several months. It's important not to allow a physician to perform a TURP to relieve urinary retention while the seeds are still active, because the retention will usually resolve on its own.

Will I need medication afterward?

Patients get a few prescriptions after the implant, including one for an antibiotic and one for an alpha-blocker. Alpha-blockers relax the bladder neck so that it's easier to urinate. The majority of patients use alpha-blockers for a few months. Some patients, however, require maintenance alpha-blockers for periods greater than one year.

The medical team may also advise patients to take an over-the-counter anti-inflammatory such as Aleve or Motrin for a short time. As an alternative, some doctors prescribe a new class of anti-inflammatory medications called COX-2 inhibitors (Vioxx or Celebrex), particularly in patients already on blood thinners such as Coumadin.

Is it true that I can start walking around within 24 hours?

Yes. Patients can be up and about when the anesthesia wears off. In fact, they usually walk out of the center a few hours after the implant.

If I travel to a center of excellence away from my home for this procedure, will long-distance air travel be a concern after brachytherapy?

Long-distance air travel should not present any problems for implant patients. However, doctors may ask their out-of-town patients to stay in town for a day or two after the procedure.

The only precaution that we recommend during a long flight goes for anyone who has to spend hours in a plane. Get up and walk around the cabin every few hours to exercise the lower leg muscles to help prevent possible blood clots. Additionally, sit in an aisle seat (this will help you stretch your legs), avoid coffee, and each time you get up to walk about the cabin go to the restroom to urinate. Be sure to use the restroom prior to landing, too.

Are there any immediate follow-up procedures after the implant?

At anytime from the day of the implant to 30 days afterward, a CT scan or MRI of the prostate is performed to make sure the prostate is receiving the proper amount of radiation. (Figure 8.3 is an x-ray view of seeds in the prostate.) If there is a significant cold spot, the doctor will contact the patient to discuss options, including the possibility of having a sec-

FIGURE 8.3   Completed Seed Implant

This is an x-ray picture of seeds in the prostate.

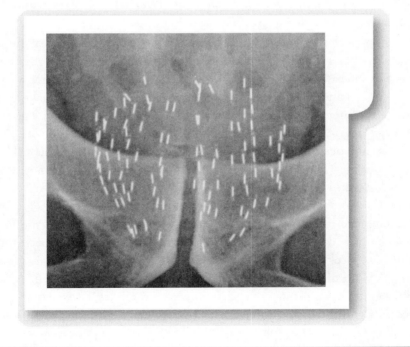

ond implant to put in a few additional seeds or undergo supplemental external beam radiation. Fortunately, this is rare. Also, a chest x-ray may be done to see if any seeds have migrated to the lung.

How does the seed get from the prostate to the lung, and is this dangerous?

In some patients, a seed will accidentally be deposited into one of the many veins that surround the prostate. The blood can carry the seed to a lung, where it can lodge and develop a two- to three-millimeter scar. There is no evidence to suggest that seed migration is harmful. If this migration does occur, it's usually in the first four weeks after the implant. There have been no reports of problems from migrated seeds and certainly the seed does not have to be removed. Nevertheless, if you are concerned about seed migration you can request seeds that are connected with absorbable suture material; these migrate less frequently.

When can I resume my regular physical activities—strength training, running, bicycle riding, and horseback riding?

When men can resume their normal activities depends on how strenuous the activities are and how they react to the implant. Most of the time, patients can ease back into their daily exercise routines in one to three weeks.

Some patients actually get themselves in trouble because they get too active too soon. Take it easy for a week or two. That means no vigorous exercise. It's okay to do light yard work, get up and walk around with your spouse, and possibly even go golfing or hit a few tennis balls if you feel like it. *If something hurts or your urination gets worse after an activity, stop doing it.* Again, take it easy for the first couple of weeks no matter what your activities. One of our patients was feeling so fit that one week after his implant he competed in a five-kilometer open water swim race. He won the race, but later that day went into urinary retention and required a catheter for a couple of weeks.

A word of caution: if you participate in activities that require straddling or bouncing—riding bicycles, horses, motorcycles, farm tractors, and the like, the bouncing motion jars the prostate. This can cause pain, swelling, and urinary problems that could result in temporary catheterization. How long patients have to avoid these activities depends on the vigor of the jarring and on each patient's individual anatomy and prostate sensitivity. Usually it's recommended that patients avoid all activities that apply pressure between the legs for the first month or two after the implant. If patients are doing well with few urinary symptoms after one month, they might try to go for a short bicycle ride or horseback ride of about 10 or 15 minutes. They would then wait 24 hours to see whether this short period of activity has worsened their urination or not. If patients notice that their urinary stream is thinner and less forceful, they should continue to avoid these activities for an additional month and then try it again. However, if there is no adverse effect on urination, they are probably ready to resume these activities.

Am I "radioactive" after the procedure?

The radiation emitted by the seeds does not cause any part of a patient's body or any of the bodily fluids to become radioactive. The radiation is of such low energy that almost all of it has dissipated before it even reaches the patient's skin. Sensitive radiation detectors can pick up minute amounts of radiation that are emitted from the body. (Note that a physics document should be prepared for patients who travel, since most airports and some train stations are equipped with radiation detectors.)

Men don't need to take special precautions with their spouses; sleeping in the same bed is fine. One study measured the dose of radiation received by the wives of 59 seed patients during a one-year period. The average dose was equivalent to taking a round-trip airline flight between New York and Tokyo.

As soon as a man feels able, he may resume sexual intercourse. Occasionally patients pass seeds with ejaculation. This is why some centers suggest patients should wear a condom or masturbate for the first three to five ejaculations.

Initial ejaculations may be uncomfortable, and the fluid could be dark brown, black, or red. This is normal and comes from bleeding that occurred during the implant.

What are seed implant's short-term effects on erectile function?

Prostatic swelling, irritation, and discomfort may reduce erectile function right after the procedure. If the patient is still experiencing erectile dysfunction after the immediate side effects wear off (usually two to three months), the usual first step is a prescription of Viagra. There is increasing evidence that to maintain erections, frequency of erections is important so that's why we encourage men to get at least three erections per week. If the patient is able to be sexually active with the help of Viagra following implant, in time he may recover the ability to achieve erections and no longer need the drug. Viagra is effective in about 80 percent of patients who have erectile dysfunction from external beam radiation or seed implant.

What precautions should I take around other family members?

Although the dose from the implant to the body's surface is very low, we recommend a few extra measures if you're around growing children or pregnant women after the implant. It's fine to be in the same room, and if you keep a distance of six feet they will get no more radiation than they would normally get from the environment (this is called background radiation). If you are closer than six feet, they will get a dose of radiation that is slightly higher than background. Remember, the average dose the spouse of an implant patient got after a whole year of exposure was equivalent to the amount of radiation passengers experience on a round-trip jet flight between New York and Tokyo.

To be extra safe, children should not sit on your lap for two months following an iodine seed implant and for three weeks following an implant of palladium seeds.

If I pass a seed during urination, what should I do with it?

Retrieve it with tweezers or a Q-tip, wrap it in aluminum foil, and return it to the radiation oncologist at the center where your implant occurred. If you mistakenly flush the seed down the toilet, don't worry. You're not going to make the town's wastewater system radioactive.

9

What Happens After the Implant? Side Effects and PSA

Deborah A. Kuban, M.D.; W. Robert Lee, M.D.;
Jay L. Friedland, M.D.; John E. Sylvester, M.D.

REGARDLESS OF WHICH treatment you choose, you're going to have to deal with temporary problems—side effects—that occur during the healing process. Before we get into the specific side effects of implants, let's take a moment to offer some basic definitions. Patients and doctors will often have different definitions of these terms, but both refer to difficulties patients may have following their procedure.

Side effects are temporary and expected. They occur because of the action of the treatment. For instance, one side effect of seeding is frequent urination, which lasts for a few months while the swelling of the prostate that occurs during the procedure and the radiation is active. This usually resolves on its own after the swelling goes down and the radiation dissipates.

Complications can have a couple of different meanings. The first connotation is an adverse event that is permanent—such as frequent urination that does not go away after the radiation has dissipated. Another general definition is a problem that occurs for the first time quite a while after the procedure. An example would be rectal bleeding (seeing blood in the toilet after having a bowel movement), which can begin a year or more after the implant procedure.

Chapter 8 described the seeding procedure and a patient's experience immediately afterward. In this chapter, we focus on the side effects and complications of brachytherapy that may happen weeks or months after the procedure.

Urinary Side Effects

How long after brachytherapy does "urgency" arise and how long does it continue?

It's almost universal that patients will experience urinary side effects for a while after seeding. These side effects are usually frequent urination, a sense of urgency, and a slower and weaker urinary stream. They are most prominent in the first few months and gradually resolve as the swelling after the implant subsides and the seeds' radiation decays.

There are two phases of irritation that may result in urinary urgency. The initial sense of needing to urinate *right now* arises just after the procedure. It's because of swelling and irritation to the prostate from the needles being inserted into the gland, the catheter, and possibly the cystoscope inserted through the urethra and into the bladder for a quick double-check of the bladder after the procedure. This irritation takes about a week or two to diminish and then things are improved for a short time. Just when you think you're over the problems, the urinary urgency begins anew. This time, it's from the radiation. The peak time for this urgency is during the strongest release of radiation, which is usually from two to six weeks after the implant. Patients may have to plan their activities around their urinations during this time, so they are not caught with an urgent need to urinate and no way to relieve themselves.

Radiation treatment also causes a number of reactions in the prostate, urethra, and lower portion of the bladder, which may take several months to resolve even after the radiation is gone. For this reason, many patients do experience some degree of side effects after a seed implant that may extend out to a year or more but finally disappear in nearly everyone. Most patients find that their urinary function recovers completely and is as good as it was before the seed implant.

How many patients develop acute urinary retention after seed implant?

There are many studies looking at this question, and depending on which one you read it can be as low as 2 percent or higher than 30 percent. However, it's widely accepted that between 5 percent and 15 percent of patients might need a catheter or other treatment for urinary retention after implant.[13] The usual number most physicians quote when a patient asks this question is 10 percent.

Is there anything I can do to prevent accidents during these first few weeks?

Yes. Some patients line their underwear with a maxi pad until the symptoms resolve. Another strategy is to avoid foods and beverages that irritate the bladder. Be sure to drink plenty of water during the day. This helps dilute the urine and make it less irritating as it passes through the urethra. Some patients who take trips during which there will be long stretches of time between bathroom breaks wear disposable pads or fitted disposable briefs, just in case.

Must I Follow a Special Diet?

Note: Though we have included suggestions on which foods may aggravate bladder irritation, there may be another dietary strategy your physician recommends. Before starting this or any other food regimen, be sure to check with your own doctor.

Some foods and liquids can irritate the bladder and prostate, causing increased urgency, frequency, discomfort, and a slower stream. The most offending foods are alcohol, citrus foods (including vitamin C), caffeinated beverages (especially coffee), and hot, spicy foods. Once you are better, begin adding things back into your daily diet one food item at a time. This way, if something does cause a flare-up, you'll be able to identify what it is.

For the first few months after the implant, be sure to drink a lot of water. This dilutes the urine and makes it more comfortable as it passes through the urethra.

Food and Beverages That May Cause Bladder Irritation

The foods items listed below are very likely to be bladder irritants in many or most people.

- Alcoholic beverages
- Apple juice
- Apples
- Cantaloupes
- Carbonated beverages
- Chilies/spicy food
- Chocolate
- Citrus fruits and drinks
- Coffee, including decaf
- Cranberries and cranberry juice
- Grapes and grape juice
- Guava
- Peaches
- Pineapple
- Plums
- Strawberries
- Tea
- Tomatoes
- Vinegar
- Vitamin B complex
- Vitamin C

Additional Foods That May Cause Bladder Irritation

These foods may be irritating to some but perhaps not the majority of people.

- Avocados
- Bananas
- Brewer's yeast

- Canned figs
- Champagne
- Cheese (aged)
- Chicken livers
- Corned beef
- Fava beans
- Lima beans
- Mayonnaise
- Nutrasweet
- Nuts
- Onions
- Pickled herring
- Prunes
- Raisins
- Rye bread
- Saccharine
- Sour cream
- Soy sauce
- Wine
- Yogurt

Substitutions

- **Low-acid fruits:** Pears, apricots, papayas, watermelon

- **For coffee drinkers:** KAVA (low-acid instant), Pero

- **For tea drinkers:** Noncitrus herbal tea or sun-brewed tea

- **Vitamin C:** Buffered ascorbic acid

- **Dietary substitutions:** Small amounts of cooked or raw green onions are allowed; processed cheese (American, cottage, cream cheese, and ricotta); carob or white chocolate instead of chocolate; homegrown low-acid tomatoes; imitation sour cream; pine nuts; freezer jams and jellies that don't require lemon juice to set the pectin

Is it important to keep the stools soft after an implant?
Yes, the first two months after the implant, take extra care to keep the stools soft. This is because a hard stool could press part of the rectal wall up against the prostate, thus increasing the dose of radiation to that part of the rectum and perhaps increasing the risk of radiation proctitis. Metamucil, Citrucel, or similar agents work well in keeping the stools soft. Similarly, beans and high gas-forming foods should be avoided for one month after palladium implants and three months after iodine seeds.

What part does age play in incontinence after implantation?
Fortunately, incontinence is rare following seed implants. The fact is that older men are more likely than younger men to experience incontinence—regardless of whether they are being treated for prostate cancer. By some definitions, 5 percent of men (age 70) are incontinent prior to receiving treatment. Therefore, elderly men with preexisting urinary symptoms will probably have more problems with incontinence after any prostate cancer treatment, including seed implant.

When it comes to urinating after the seeding procedure, I've heard that nighttime is worse than daytime. Is there an explanation for this?
It's common for an older man to experience a strong urine stream during the day and a weaker one at night, regardless of whether he has been or is currently being treated for prostate cancer.

    Upon lying down at night, fluids pool in the central body and stretch blood vessels in the chest. This stretching sends signals to the body to make more urine, which subsequently increases the frequency of nighttime urination. Also at night, the involuntary nervous system (the autonomic system) can slightly inhibit the bladder from completely emptying. That's why when you try to urinate, your stream may be slower and there could be a feeling of not being quite done. This incomplete emptying means the bladder refills more quickly and you probably have to get out of bed again to urinate, sometimes several times.

How can I alleviate nighttime urinary problems?
Alpha-blocker medications such as Flomax, Hytrin, and Cardura help counteract these problems by helping the urethra to relax, which allows for more

complete emptying. Also, refrain from drinking any beverages for about three to four hours before going to bed. When watching television or engaging in other quiet evening activities, it's a good idea to put your feet up. This will help the fluids that have collected in the lower extremities work their way back up and be urinated out of the body before retiring.

It's also a good idea to try to empty the bladder completely before going to bed. Taking a warm shower in the night may help the flow, and walking around prior to urination can sometimes improve the stream.

A small percentage of patients are permanently left with a bit more sensitive bladder, meaning they may have to get up more often at night to urinate, it's difficult to postpone urination when the urge occurs and the urinary stream is weaker.

Will I ever leak when coughing, straining, or having sex like many men do who have had their prostates surgically removed?

One of the benefits of seed implants is that the specific problem of leaking urine is very rare. Stress incontinence, which is weakness of the pelvic muscles that causes leakage with coughing, straining, or exercise, is also exceedingly rare after seeds.

The second type of incontinence is known as urge incontinence. This is when patients who experience extreme urgency find themselves leaking a bit of urine if they can't find a bathroom in time. After seed implantation, you may have this urge type of incontinence for the first few weeks, or even months, but it usually goes away.

Are Kegel exercises recommended with seed implantation?

Kegel exercises strengthen the muscles that help to keep the urethra closed, thus improving incontinence and urine control (see Chapter 6). Incontinence isn't as much of a problem with seeds as it is with surgery, but many physicians think it's a good idea to practice Kegel exercises if the patient is experiencing any degree of incontinence.

Are there surgical procedures that may help incontinence?

Yes, but these surgeries are seldom necessary after a seed implant. Our advice is to stay away from any sort of surgical procedure for incontinence until the side effects from the implant have decreased. If you are considering surgery to the prostate or bladder for any reason, consult your brachytherapist *before* you have it. Having surgery too early can make the incontinence worse in the long run.

What if my urologist recommends that I have a transurethral resection of the prostate (TURP) after implantation?

The worry about doing any surgical procedure in the prostate or urethra following seeding is that the radiation may cause some scarring, making it more difficult for any surgical trauma to heal. Because of this, we recommend surgery be avoided unless absolutely necessary; the longer you can wait to have this kind of surgery following a seed implant, the better.

However, some patients need some type of procedure to open up their prostate if they've had troublesome, persistent blockage symptoms that medication fails to relieve. Following the principle of doing the least amount of surgery possible, a transurethral incision of the prostate (TUIP) is often recommended. This is less traumatic than a TURP and can often relieve the obstruction. A TURP can be done after seeds, but it's recommended that only a small amount of tissue be removed, which is often called a "mini-TURP."

A patient should wait at least six to nine months after brachytherapy before undergoing a TUIP or mini-TURP. This time period allows the radiation to dissipate and the tissue to heal. Frequently, the urinary side effects resolve on their own. We reiterate: *prior to having any surgery performed on the prostate, bladder, or rectum after an implant, contact your brachytherapist.*

If I had benign prostatic hyperplasia (BPH) prior to seeding, will it go away or return later?

Following seed implantation, the prostate will gradually become smaller during a period of several years. There is no evidence that the prostate regrows later, and patients followed as long as 15 years after their implant have not noted any re-enlargement of their prostate.

Some patients with BPH have greatly enlarged prostates but few urinary symptoms. Conversely, there are men whose BPH has caused only a little bit of prostate enlargement yet they have striking urinary difficulties. Thus, there's not always a correlation between the size of the patient's enlarged prostate and the amount of trouble he may have. Similarly, there's no way to predict whether your BPH symptoms will improve after seeding. Simply stated, some patients who have BPH-related symptoms improve over the years after an implant, while others do not. We can't foresee who those will be.

I've noticed a burning sensation 8 to 12 months after I had the seed implants. Do other men experience it? What causes it and how is it treated?

A small percentage of patients complain of this. There are several possibilities including bacterial infection, which is treated by antibiotics, or cystitis/urethritis, which is usually treated with other medications.

Occasionally, burning and increased urinary frequency develop one to three years after brachytherapy. This can be due to a small stricture (scar tissue) that may develop in the urethra. If this occurs, cystoscopy—an outpatient procedure to widen (dilate) the urethra—is usually effective in treating this problem.

Bowel Side Effects

Will I have any side effects to the bowel after the implant?

Because a very small portion of the rectum receives radiation, it's rare for patients to experience any rectal or bowel side effects from a seed implant alone. Some patients, however, notice that their bowel movements are a little more irregular and frequent for a few weeks following the implant. This effect usually disappears rapidly.

Up to 15 percent of patients will have minor rectal bleeding either seen on the toilet tissue or with the stool. Typically, it doesn't hurt, the amount of bleeding is usually insignificant, and it usually gets better on its own. Occasionally, it will require a prescription for a suppository or another minor treatment. On rare occasions, a seed patient may report a burning sensation during defecation, which can be treated with medication.

Patients who receive external beam radiation with seed implants have a slightly greater chance of temporary rectal or bowel side effects. These side effects tend to come on a bit later. This group of patients also shows a greater incidence of developing more permanent bowel problems or a tendency for diarrhea. Note that with the advent of intensity modulated radiation therapy (IMRT), there is less bowel or rectal toxicity during and after treatment.

Can bowel side effects show up later?

There are some brachytherapy patients (although it's a much smaller percentage than external beam patients) who develop some blood in their stools about a year or two after the implant. This is usually caused by some slight fragility to the lining of the rectum.

Any rectal bleeding that occurs months after the implant needs to be reported to the doctor immediately. The physician will probably recommend that colonoscopy be performed to rule out anything serious. Most of the time, this bleeding will go away on its own.

We advise that any procedure to the rectum after brachytherapy be conservative. Simple prescription suppositories that help accelerate the body's normal healing process should be the first-line treatment. We recommend that implant patients do not undergo electrocautery because it might create an ulceration or fistula. Likewise, performing a biopsy on an area of radiation proctitis can result in a fistula or ulcer that does not heal. That's why we advise that the patient talk with his brachytherapist before undergoing any invasive procedure to deal with minor rectal bleeding after brachytherapy.

Sexual Function

What does radiation from the seeds do to the prostate?

You will probably experience a significant reduction in the ejaculate. This is because radiation affects the seminal vesicles producing prostatic fluid. Also, as the normal cells die, the prostate becomes smaller, shrinking to about half its normal size. When your doctor performs a digital rectal exam (DRE) after your implant, he or she will notice that over time the prostate comes to feel small and flat.

One man I talked to said his prostate continued to shrink well into the second and third year after treatment. Why does the prostate continue to shrink after the radiation has dissipated?

The radiation effect on both cancerous and noncancerous cells is subtle and takes a long time. Although noncancerous prostate cells are damaged immediately when radiation is given, the cells can continue to live for many months or even years. For the cells to die from the radiation damage, it requires them to attempt to divide into two cells. Prostate cancer cells and noncancerous prostate cells divide at their own rate so it can take a long time before full shrinkage of the prostate is seen. It's been observed that in some patients, it took up to five years for most of the normal prostate to disappear following the radiation treatment. This is an indication of how slowly radiation works and that it takes time for the prostate to shrink to its smallest size. Not all prostates will shrink radically. The amount and rate of prostate shrinkage has no bearing on controlling the cancer.

What about long-term sexual problems?

There's controversy and debate about what exactly causes erectile dysfunction after brachytherapy. It has been speculated that it could be due to radiation's effect on the nearby nerves or the effect on the blood vessels that supply an erection.

A recent study shows that one year after the implant, 90 percent of men who had good erectile function prior to the procedure maintained erectile function. About half of these patients reported some decrease in the erection's firmness or durability but were still able to penetrate with the help of Viagra.

Long-term effects on erectile function occur over a period of years. After five years, 50 percent of brachytherapy patients maintain the same erectile function as they had before seeds. In addition, these brachytherapy patients are, on average, 10 to 15 years older than patients that undergo nerve-sparing prostatectomy, as reported in the medical literature.

It's recognized that men who have other medical problems that tend to affect their blood vessel system will have weaker erections. These are conditions such as diabetes, arteriosclerosis, and a history of heavy smoking. Older men are more likely to have these medical problems, and if they do, they are more susceptible to erectile dysfunction following treatment. Lastly, many prescription medications cause erectile dysfunction.

I've heard that some men's penises shrink after prostate cancer treatment. Is this true?

The penis length can appear to shrink after radical prostatectomy. This has to do with cutting out the part of the urethra that runs through the prostate; shortening the urethra can shorten the penis. A few patients who had either external beam radiation or brachytherapy have also reported a shortening of their penises. It's not clearly understood why this occurs. Since many men have fewer erections after cancer treatment, this has been speculated to be the cause of penile shrinkage.

What are the changes in ejaculate as a result of brachytherapy? How is this different from changes that occur in ejaculate because of radical prostatectomy?

Most of the fluid that makes up the ejaculate is made in the prostate and seminal vesicles. Following radical prostatectomy, patients can climax but they do not ejaculate since the surgery removes both the prostate and the seminal vesicles.

Following brachytherapy, the amount of the ejaculate is often diminished. The small amount of ejaculate is thought to come from the distal portions of the seminal vesicles, which are not implanted. About 5 percent to 10 percent of men have completely "dry ejaculations" after brachytherapy. Most have significantly reduced volume. Approximately 5 percent of patients have no change in ejaculate volume.

Will there be pain during ejaculation?

A small number of patients report discomfort, particularly with the first few ejaculations. The reason for the pain is probably due to swelling or some slight scarring of the ejaculatory ducts. This pain usually subsides with subsequent ejaculations.

Does radiation affect sperm? What happens when that sperm fertilizes an egg? Does it affect the offspring?

Although it is thought the testicles can continue to produce sperm after the seed implant, there is a remote possibility that the radiation will affect these sperm. We recommend attempts to impregnate be avoided for at least 18 months. However, since the nature and quality of the ejaculate is dramatically altered by the seed radiation, it is unlikely that a patient would be fertile. This, however, is not a guarantee—on occasion, men are still fertile following this procedure. In fact, some radiation oncologists have had patients who successfully fathered healthy children after their prostate seed implant.

If you are a younger patient and are concerned about the ability to father children, consider sperm banking prior to the seed implant.

The Prostate Specific Antigen (PSA) Level

When should my PSA level be checked following the seed implant? How often should I get it checked?
Your PSA levels can actually increase immediately after the implant because anything that irritates the prostate (trauma, infection, cancer, or inflammation) will temporarily increase the PSA level. How often the PSA should be checked after implant varies from doctor to doctor and may depend somewhat on how the PSA acts following therapy. In general, we like to see a PSA test done every three to six months until the PSA reaches a low, stable level.

Do you use the surgical standard for PSA after brachytherapy?
The surgical standard is 0.2 ng/mL. It may take years for the PSA to reach its lowest level after radiation. In one case, it took seven years for a patient's PSA to drop to 0.2 ng/mL.

Rather than a strict rule about the PSA needing to decline to a specific and relatively arbitrary level, there is another well-accepted standard used by brachytherapists, urologists, and radiation oncologists to monitor what's happening after the implant. When the PSA falls to a low level after brachytherapy and stays put for successive readings (barring the PSA bounce phenomena, which we discuss later) the patient is considered disease-free (or progression-free) by PSA criteria.

If I still have a measurable PSA, does this mean I still have prostate cancer?
No. A low PSA level does not mean there's prostate cancer. It could simply reflect the fact that the few remaining normal prostate cells continue to pro-

duce PSA. A small amount of PSA may be seen not only after implant, but after surgery or external beam radiation as well.

What PSA level should be hoped for over the long term?

While PSA levels would be expected to decrease to a level of less than 1.0 ng/mL, the absolute level is not as important as the trend over time. Prostate specific antigen levels should slowly decline over several years and then stabilize. There is no set standard for an absolute PSA value because every man is different. One patient's PSA could be 0.5 ng/mL, while the patient sitting next to him in the waiting room could have a PSA of 0.7 ng/mL, and yet another patient could have a PSA of 0.2 ng/mL. The important factor for each of these men is that his PSA has reached its lowest point and is not rising.

It's not unheard of for a small number of brachytherapy patients to have stable PSA levels above 1 ng/mL. In general, however, the lower the PSA, the better. Long-term studies have demonstrated that patients whose lowest PSA is less than 1 ng/mL have more than a 90 percent chance of being free of prostate cancer 10 years after implantation.

Will my PSA reading be steady after the procedure, or will it fluctuate?

Approximately 24 percent to 40 percent of patients will experience a PSA bounce (also referred to as a spike or blip), which means the PSA temporarily goes up and then declines. This usually happens between 12 and 36 months after implant. The magnitude of this rise can be a few tenths of a point or several points. The PSA of one of our patients rose to 13 ng/mL and then dropped right back down. About one-quarter of these bounce patients will have a second PSA bounce from a few months to a few years after the first PSA bounce.

Researchers haven't yet been able to ascertain what causes the PSA bounce. It may be due to normal cells that are dying and releasing their PSA, inflammation, or a mild infection. Because the PSA bounce *may* be due to an infection or swelling, your doctor might prescribe antibiotics or an anti-inflammatory medication.

If the PSA bounce occurs, what should I do?

If your PSA is up during a routine follow-up visit, the normal course of action would be for your doctor to repeat the PSA in two to three months.

While many bounces are of short duration, some last many months, during which time the PSA is carefully monitored.

Interestingly, physicians have noted that more frequently it's the younger men who have PSA bounces and their bounces are higher. Perhaps it's because they have more normal, healthy prostate cells and when their larger number of cells die, they produce a bigger, temporary PSA bounce. That could explain why a man in his 40s may experience a PSA bounce that's much higher than a man in his 70s. Our advice for both these men is not to worry. Get retested in two to three months.

There are two other things seed implant patients need to know about PSA fluctuations. The PSA test results can vary according to the laboratory performing them. Therefore, it's wise for a patient to ask his doctor to make sure to send each PSA test to the same lab. And, ejaculation can also temporarily increase a man's PSA level. That's why sexual activity should be avoided for two days prior to any PSA test.

If my PSA rises after implant, should I have a biopsy?

There really is no need to perform postimplant prostate biopsies within two years after the procedure. Biopsies in the first couple of years are likely to be inaccurate because many cells are biologically alive but reproductively dead—the cancerous cells look alive under a microscope but they are incapable of reproducing.

If the PSA begins to rise after about two years, your doctor will assess whether to do a biopsy. Biopsies are most often performed to determine if the recurrent cancer is local (within the prostate).

If the PSA rise is rapid, a biopsy may not be ordered. This is because a rapidly rising PSA is a signal that the patient may have distant spread (prostate cancer that has migrated to some other site in the body). Taking out the prostate won't cure this cancer. In these cases, hormones would be the usual next step.

Another circumstance in which a biopsy might not be ordered when the PSA starts to rise after seeding is when the patient is elderly. Salvage therapy—a second treatment such as surgery or cryosurgery—to deal with a local recurrence can take an extra physical toll on older patients. That's why patients of advanced age and/or in poor health are often better candidates for hormonal therapy in this kind of situation.

If the cancer returns in the prostate after implant, what can I do?
For well-selected patients who are in the hands of an experienced
brachytherapist, the chance of local recurrence is low. If you do have recurrent prostate cancer, your doctor will take a good amount of time discussing
possible treatment choices based on your age, general medical condition,
initial tumor stage, initial tumor grade, PSA doubling time, prostate biopsy
results, and results of workup to determine if it's metastatic disease.

In the process of selecting a treatment the first time around, some
physicians tell men, "If you have had radiation to the prostate and the cancer comes back, you can never have a prostatectomy." This is not entirely
true. Removing the prostate after radiation (salvage prostatectomy) can be
done, but it's very difficult and the success rates are rather low. Only a few
surgeons in the United States have sufficient experience to do it and the rate
of incontinence can be as high as 50 percent.

Besides salvage prostatectomy, other options in the event of recurrence
after seeding include salvage brachytherapy (another brachytherapy procedure), cryosurgery, hormonal treatment, investigational/experimental drugs
or procedures, or even watchful waiting. These options are discussed in
more detail in Chapter 11.

10

Will I Have to Be on Hormones?

Celestia S. Higano, M.D.; Ian M. Thompson, M.D.;
John E. Sylvester, M.D.

THE THERAPIES DISCUSSED so far—surgery, external beam radiation, and seeds—treat cancer that is in or near the prostate. But what if the cells are scattered throughout the body because the prostate cancer has spread? In this setting, hormonal therapy plays an important role.

There are numerous names for hormonal therapy, including hormone treatment, endocrine therapy, hormonal ablation, testosterone ablation, androgen ablation, androgen deprivation treatment, and even castration. In the past, this treatment was reserved for men with metastatic prostate cancer. However, because of the range of drugs available today, we can start hormonal therapy much earlier, combining it with other treatments to help fight disease that is locally advanced but not obviously metastatic. On occasion, we may even use hormones in patients with early stage disease.

Hormonal therapy is a complex topic that by itself would fill hundreds of pages. Our goal in this chapter is to give you a broad overview so that if your doctor brings up the possibility of hormonal therapy, you will have a basic understanding of how it works and its potential side effects. With this knowledge, you can talk further with your physician to determine if hormone therapy is the right choice for you.

Hormonal Therapy Basics

How does hormone therapy work?

Most testosterone comes from the testicles. The adrenal glands make a small amount of testosterone as well as other male hormones. These other hormones are called adrenal androgens. The term "androgen" is used to describe the entire group of male hormones.

The aim of hormonal therapy is to reduce the amount of testosterone and androgens in the bloodstream, depriving many prostate cancer cells of the fuel they need to grow. Once the male hormones are withdrawn, one of three things will happen to a prostate cancer cell: it will undergo spontaneous death (called apoptosis), it will remain alive but not grow, or it will keep right on growing. Cells in this last category are called androgen-independent prostate cancer cells because they don't need androgens to grow.

Reducing testosterone usually lowers the prostate specific antigen (PSA), shrinks the prostate, shrinks the tumor, or stops the progress of the disease—frequently for many years. Generally speaking, however, hormone therapy alone does not cure prostate cancer.

Interfering with Testosterone

Is there more than one way to interfere with testosterone?

Yes. There are four primary ways to interfere with testosterone: surgically removing the testicles (orchiectomy), using drugs to interrupt testosterone production (luteinizing hormone-releasing hormone [LHRH] agonists ketoconazole and aminoglutethimide), using drugs that block androgen action (antiandrogens), and taking estrogen.

Surgery

- **Orchiectomy.** Surgical removal of the testicles (orchiectomy) was for many years the only way to reduce testosterone. It's used less frequently today, though, because of the availability of hormonal therapy medications. When orchiectomy is done, it's usually an outpatient procedure. The surgeon makes a small incision into the scrotum and removes the testicles. Immediately, testosterone declines to a very low level called the castrate range. (The scrotum remains, and if the patient opted for reconstructive surgery prior to undergoing orchiectomy, the surgeon inserts prostheses shaped like testicles.)

The advantage of orchiectomy is that it's a very economical way to reduce testosterone. There is no need for the patient to receive regular doses of hormone-blocking medications. The disadvantage is that the operation is irreversible.

Drugs That Interrupt Testosterone Production

• **LHRH agonists.** Testosterone production begins in the hypothalamus, which is a portion of the brain controlling numerous bodily functions. The pituitary gland sits directly beneath the hypothalamus. When the testosterone level in the blood falls below a certain threshold, the hypothalamus sends LHRH to the pituitary gland. The pituitary then sends another set of chemical signals to the testicles. The testicles go to work and produce testosterone.

The group of drugs known as LHRH agonists breaks this cycle at the very beginning by turning off the hypothalamus's production of LHRH. The most frequently used LHRH agonists are given as injections and last between one and four months. After the injection, it takes about three weeks for the testosterone to fall to the castrate range. The primary advantage of these drugs is that the testosterone reduction is temporary, so stopping the drug means most of the side effects will probably disappear. In some men, because of an initial increase in testosterone after the first injection, the physician will add a second oral antiandrogen medication for several weeks to block this effect.

• **Prevention of androgen production.** There is another group of drugs that prevent the testicles from making testosterone and the adrenal glands from making androgens. These drugs include ketoconazole and aminoglutethimide. These drugs are not usually used as first-line hormonal therapy treatment but are more commonly used to treat hormone-refractory prostate cancer (this is when prostate cancer no longer responds to other types of hormonal therapy). These drugs are often used as second-line hormonal therapy before undertaking chemotherapy.

Drugs That Prevent Androgen Action

- **Antiandrogens.** Inside prostate cancer cells are structures called androgen receptors. Androgens in the bloodstream bind to these receptors
and when they do, it's like flipping a switch that causes the cancer cells
to grow. Antiandrogen drugs increase androgen levels in the bloodstream. But, they also plug into the receptors so that androgens in the
bloodstream can't. With antiandrogens blocking the receptors, the
male hormones are unable to turn on the switch.

  In some cases, some practitioners treat low- and intermediate-risk
patients with early prostate cancer solely with antiandrogens. For
younger patients especially, this approach may reduce the risk of erectile dysfunction. Though there may be some quality of life benefits to
using antiandrogens alone, this approach requires further study. (For
high-risk patients, however, antiandrogen monotherapy is usually not
recommended.)

  Antiandrogens can, and often are, used in combination with
LHRH agonists. The very first dose of LHRH agonist causes a brief,
sharp increase in testosterone before the testosterone drops to castrate
levels. Such a rapid increase in testosterone can cause a painful "tumor
flare" if there's cancer in the bone. Since the antiandrogen plugs up the
androgen receptors, it helps prevent this "flare."

  There are a few names for the dual treatment with LHRH agonists and antiandrogens—combined hormonal therapy, total androgen
blockade, or complete hormonal blockade. Men on total androgen
blockade tend to experience more side effects than those taking a single hormonal agent.

Estrogen

Estrogen is a hormone that can interfere with testosterone production. For
years, higher doses of diethylstilbestrol (DES)—a synthetic form of estrogen—were used to treat prostate cancer as an alternative to orchiectomy.
These doses are not recommended today because of the availability of the
LHRH agonists. At higher doses, DES increases the chance of developing
serious heart disease or blood clots. Lower doses are often used to treat
hormone-refractory prostate cancer. One advantage to DES is that it is

effective and very inexpensive. There are also other estrogen-containing pills or patches.

When Is Hormone Therapy Used?

Isn't hormone therapy used only in cases of metastatic cancer?

That's the way it was done in the past. This is because orchiectomy—an irreversible operation—was the best way to control testosterone levels. But with LHRH agonists and antiandrogen drugs—whose effects *are* reversible—hormonal therapy is no longer just for men with metastatic prostate cancer. That's why if you have other stages of prostate cancer your doctor might recommend hormonal therapy along with radiation or surgery.

Are men with early stage prostate cancer ever treated with just hormones?

Occasionally. Although hormones can control prostate cancer for many years, hormonal therapy by itself generally does not cure it. Because hormones have so many side effects and there are other excellent curative treatments, it's uncommon to give hormones alone to early stage patients. When it's used alone for early prostate cancer, it's usually for elderly patients who cannot tolerate conventional treatments such as surgery, seed implantation, or external beam radiation.

Are hormones used before radical prostatectomy?

Here's a quick explanation of the theory behind this practice. When prostate cancer is confined to the organ, survival rates tend to be better than when there is a positive surgical margin or extracapsular extension. Since hormonal therapy shrinks cancer cells, the idea is to shrink the tumor so that it is completely inside the prostate. Unfortunately, hormonal therapy for three to eight months before surgery has not resulted in improved outcomes.

If the pathology report after surgery shows positive margins, will I need hormones?

The question of whether you will have hormones in the case of positive margins probably boils down to where you get your treatment. Physicians at some centers advocate no treatment unless the margins are strongly positive. In this case, a common treatment is radiation therapy.

On the other hand, doctors at other facilities say even if the margins are not strongly positive, the patient still needs aggressive therapy, including hormones and radiation. But this is not yet proven to be superior to radiation alone.

There are many factors to consider in the case of positive margins: the extent of the positive margins, whether the cancer extended into the seminal vesicles, the Gleason score, the PSA level before and after surgery, and the patient's willingness to undergo more treatment. Because there are so many factors, turning to your own doctor for counsel and advice is very important. You may be able to enroll in a clinical trial. (Additional information regarding an important National Cancer Institute clinical trial is available from the NCI Cancer Information Service at 1-800-4Cancer or at www.cancer.gov.)

When are hormones and external beam radiation therapy used together?

Hormones can be used before, during, and after external beam radiation therapy.

The idea behind using hormones before radiation is that the hormones may kill some cancer cells and weaken others, making them even more susceptible to the radiation. Large randomized studies show that hormone therapy before and during moderate dose radiation has significant benefits for local control and disease-free survival for locally advanced cancer. Thus, the standard of care for patients with locally advanced cancer is to combine hormone therapy and external beam radiation.

In this setting of locally advanced prostate cancer, some studies suggest that using hormones for several years is better than using them for a short time. Therefore, in treating locally advanced prostate cancer, many doctors recommend continuing hormone therapy for several years after the completion of external beam radiation therapy. However, one landmark study recently showed that two months of hormones before whole pelvic plus prostate radiation and two months during radiation therapy was effective in patients with a risk of lymph node involvement of over 15 percent and a pre-treatment PSA of under 100. So, the optimal duration of hormone use and how best to combine it in patients with locally advanced disease is still being debated. For men getting radiation for early cancer, however, there is no convincing evidence that adding hormones is helpful or necessary. Clinical trials evaluating this question are currently ongoing.

Under what circumstances are hormones used prior to seed implants?
Hormones may be used before seed implants to help shrink a prostate that's too large. We will commonly recommend three to six months of hormones to a man with an overly large prostate in order to shrink it to a more ideal size for the implant. A few months of total androgen blockade will shrink most prostates by about 40 percent.

In terms of using hormones to increase the effectiveness of implants, several studies have been published looking at the impact of a short course of hormone therapy (three to six months) combined with brachytherapy. None of these studies has shown there's a benefit in adding a few months of hormones to a seed implant.

One final thought about combining hormones and seeds: although there are no studies on this, many doctors would recommend two to three years of hormone therapy if the dual treatment of seeds and external beam radiation therapy is used for early stage, high-risk disease (high Gleason score or a high PSA).

I had another treatment a couple of years ago, but my PSA has started to climb again. How quickly should I go on hormones?
Men in this situation often live for many years without the cancer spreading to the bones or other organs. But other patients develop cancer spread in a much shorter time frame. While there's no sure way to predict which patient will have rapid spread, how fast the PSA doubles is an indicator. A rapid PSA doubling time (10 to 12 months) is more likely to be associated with a poorer outcome than a PSA doubling time of greater than one year (other factors include original PSA, stage, and Gleason score).

Many men with rising PSA want treatments that will lower the PSA under any circumstance. Moreover, some data suggest that early hormonal intervention after failed treatment, while the disease is minimal, may extend survival—but these data remain controversial. There are many clinical trials that do not include hormonal therapy, and some men choose a non-hormonal approach first and delay the use of hormonal therapy. Patients with rapid PSA doubling times should consider treatment, while those with a slower PSA doubling time can possibly delay any therapy.

What's intermittent hormonal therapy?

This is simply stopping and then re-starting hormonal therapy. It's hypothesized that this on-again, off-again use of hormones delays the development of hormone-refractory prostate cancer, but this concept is not proven. The general idea is that hormones are stopped after a given number of months of therapy or when the PSA reaches a very low level. After the hormonal therapy is stopped, the PSA is expected to rise. When the PSA rises to a certain level again, the drugs are restarted. A potential advantage of intermittent therapy is that the side effects may go away or diminish during the time off the androgen suppression. Intermittent therapy is controversial, and clinical trials looking at its effectiveness are now underway.

Side Effects

What do doctors commonly tell patients about the side effects of hormonal therapy?

Physicians commonly warn patients about loss of sex drive (libido) and the subsequent erectile dysfunction, and hot flashes.

- **Loss of libido.** Losing the desire for sex is common with orchiectomy or LHRH agonists. Only a small percentage of patients maintain their normal sexual desire. It's impossible, though, for us to predict who will retain libido. The loss of sexual desire often results in the loss of spontaneous erections.

- **Hot flashes.** A hot flash is a sudden rush of warmth to the face, neck, upper chest, and back. It lasts for a few seconds or up to an hour. They range from mild to severe (see Table 10.1). The frequency and severity are different for every man, and hot flashes can occur one or many times each day. The good news is that prescription medications can alleviate hot flashes, as may dietary additives such as soy.

Are there other side effects not always mentioned?

Yes, there may be several, depending on a man's sensitivity to the treatment and how long he's on hormones. Men can experience physical, metabolic, and physiologic changes, as well as alterations in mood and even cognitive functioning.

TABLE 10.1 Hot Flash Severity: Description of Symptoms

This chart identifies the differing levels of hot flashes, their usual duration, and the physical and possible emotional reactions one may experience.

Severity	Sensation	Duration (min)	Emotion	Physical Symptoms	Actions Required
Mild	Generalized warmth or a flushed sensation	≤ 3	Rare	None to very light perspiration	None
Moderate	More warmth and/or flushing	≤ 5	Mild anxiety or irritability; loss of concentration	Light to moderate perspiration	Fanning, loosening clothing, removing clothing or bedding
Severe	"Hotter" or "very hot"	≤ 10	Moderate anxiety or irritability	Heavy perspiration, dizziness, nausea, shortness of breath, weakness, extreme discomfort	Loosening or changing clothing and/or bedding
Very Severe	"Very hot"	≤ 30	Anxiety or irritability, restlessness, "totally out of control"	Drenching perspiration, dizziness, nausea, shortness of breath, weakness, chest discomfort, extreme discomfort	Changing clothing, changing bedding, toweling off, using wet towels, taking a bath or shower, resting

Reprinted from *Urologic Nursing*, 1994, Volume 14, Number 4, p. 156. Reprinted with permission of the publisher, the Society of Urologic Nurses and Associates, Inc. (SUNA), East Holly Avenue, Box 56, Pitman, NJ 08071-0056; (856)256-2300; Fax (856)589-7463; e-mail: uronsg@ajj.com; website: www.suna.inurse.com

- **Breast enlargement.** Some patients, particularly those on long-term hormonal therapy, may experience enlargement of the male breast tissue (called gynecomastia). This can occur with antiandrogens or LHRH analog treatments alone or in combination. Radiation is proven to be very effective at preventing or decreasing the severity of the gynecomastia if given before high-dose bicalutamide or DES. Radiation to prevent gynecomastia before LHRH analog therapy has not been studied and is not routinely performed. Although radiation can prevent breast enlargement, it does not prevent breast tenderness. Prescription drugs can be very effective in treating tender breasts.

    If gynecomastia is severe or extremely bothersome, surgery or liposuction are options. Radiation to the breast tissue will not treat gynecomastia once it has occurred.

- **Weight gain.** When on hormonal therapy, men gain an average of five to 12 pounds. There is a loss of muscle mass with an increase in total body fat, most of which accumulates in the trunk. Reversing the weight gain isn't easy, but patients can—and should—make a point of increasing their exercise and moderating their caloric intake. A proactive approach will help minimize this problem.

- **Testicle changes.** Hormonal therapy can result in a reduction in the size of the testicles. On intermittent therapy, when the hormonal therapy is stopped, the testicles may regain some, but usually not all, of their original size.

- **Loss of bone mineral density.** In one recent report, men on combined hormonal therapy of an LHRH agonist and an antiandrogen lost 4.7 percent of bone in their lower spine and 2.7 percent from their hips (this compares with the normal loss of 0.5 percent to 1 percent per year). This level of bone loss is actually greater than what postmenopausal women experience. Some men already have osteoporosis before starting hormonal therapy and they could be treated with a type of drug called a bisphosphonate to help increase bone density. You should have a DEXA (dual x-ray absorptiometry) scan to assess whether you have normal bone density before you start hormonal therapy.

If you have normal bone density, some of the best things you can do to counteract bone loss are to exercise and take calcium and vitamin D supplements (talk with your own doctor about how much you should take).

- **Anemia.** Anemia, which is a low level of red blood cells, is frequently reported as a side effect of hormonal therapy. Most patients have some anemia, but only about 10 to 15 percent develop symptoms due to a low red blood count. Drugs can be used to treat anemia during hormonal therapy. Red blood cell production resumes at more normal rates once the androgen suppression is stopped.

- **Lipid changes and aggravation of existing diseases.** Hormonal therapy tends to increase total cholesterol and the level of low-density lipoprotein (LDL)—the so-called "bad" cholesterol. Lipid levels should be monitored and if the situation warrants, your physician can prescribe cholesterol-lowering drugs.

    If hypertension (high blood pressure) and/or diabetes exist, hormonal therapy can aggravate these two conditions, although the exact mechanisms of why this happens remain unclear. If you have one of these conditions and your cancer doctor puts you on hormonal therapy, be sure to tell your primary care physician so he or she can help watch for any undue changes in your preexisting high blood pressure or diabetes.

- **Other changes.** Another patient-reported side effect is fatigue or lack of energy. As with some of the other side effects brought about by hormone therapy, we don't have a good explanation for why this happens. We do know that regular exercise, and particularly resistance exercises (free weights, weight machines, elastic tubing, calisthenics), can improve symptoms of fatigue and overall quality of life. This type of exercise should be done initially under the supervision of a physical therapist or licensed personal trainer. When hormone therapy is stopped, this fatigue usually goes away.

    Some patients are also more depressed and more moody. Again, regular exercise helps relieve this anxiety. In more severe cases, doctors can prescribe an antidepressant.

II

What Happens if the
Cancer Returns?

Celestia S. Higano, M.D.; Jay L. Friedland, M.D.;
David C. Beyer, M.D.; Katsuto Shinohara, M.D.;
John C. Blasko, M.D.

"WHAT HAPPENS IF it comes back?" That's arguably the most nagging question lurking in the back of any cancer patient's mind. For patients with early stage prostate cancer, primary treatments usually work. But the truth of the matter is that medicine has not come far enough to cure all patients.

Before we delve into the specifics of symptoms and treatments, we'd like to offer a word of reassurance. It's not uncommon for us to sometimes hear patients berate themselves when they are told their prostate cancer is back. They wonder out loud, "If I had done just one more thing, taken an alternate path, or chosen another doctor, would I have been able to avoid recurrence?"

The success rate for curing early stage prostate cancer is high. But despite the many excellent and successful curative therapies, the disease does come back in some men. Often no one knows exactly why. That's why we want patients to know that cancer recurrence *does not* happen because of something they did—or did not—do.

If you or a loved one winds up facing cancer recurrence, having an optimistic attitude will go a long way in helping you get through the therapies a second time. We encourage our patients to not only draw on their own strengths but also be open to receiving support from the people and resources around them to help meet this challenge one more time.

Recurrence Basics

Can you provide a simple explanation of local and distant cancer recurrence?

Cancer recurrence means that after the cancer was treated, usually with surgery, seeds, or external beam radiation, it has returned. If it returns in the vicinity of the prostate or prostate bed (where the prostate used to be), it's called local recurrence. It if comes back outside the immediate area, it's called distant recurrence or metastasis.

Why didn't my original treatment work?

There are so many factors that enter into a treatment decision that it's difficult to point to a single reason why the primary therapy failed. Furthermore, as we mentioned in the introduction to this chapter, the true reasons for cancer recurrence often remain unknown. However, we can offer a few potential reasons that may explain some treatment failures:

- In the case of watchful waiting, perhaps the cancer grew more quickly than anticipated and escaped the prostate and treatment area, despite thorough and frequent monitoring.
- If surgery was the primary treatment, the cancer might have recurred because some of the cancerous cells spread outside the prostate before the operation. Another possibility is that a microscopic amount of the tumor was left behind and continued to grow.
- If radiation (either brachytherapy or external beam) was the initial treatment, it could be that some of the radiation energy missed some of the cancer cells. Or perhaps some malignant cells escaped the treatment area before radiation was applied, or—and this is rare—that particular cancer was resistant to the usual doses of radiation.

Does recurrent prostate cancer mean I have cancer throughout my body?

No. Although spread outside the prostate area is a frequent cause of recurrent disease, a rise in prostate specific antigen (PSA) doesn't automatically mean the cancer has spread to other parts of the body. Recurrent prostate cancer can turn up just in the prostate after radiation or in the case of prostatectomy, in the surgical bed where the prostate used to be.

How long does it take for recurrence to show up?

The rate and timing of recurrence depends on the aggressiveness of the original cancer. High-grade cancer often recurs earlier than moderate- and low-grade cancers.

Most cases of cancer recurrence occur within the first five years, but recurrences can occur as late as 15 years after initial therapy. Most men who survive 10 years without evidence of PSA relapse are likely to be cured.

Does recurrent prostate cancer have to be treated?

This is something each man and his physician have to decide together. A study in the *Journal of the American Medical Association* clearly demonstrated that an increasing PSA does not mean the patient is at imminent risk of dying from prostate cancer.[14] More than 300 prostatectomy patients (most of whom had low-risk, favorable disease prior to surgery) with a rising PSA were followed without additional treatment for as long as 15 years. On average, in those men whose PSA began to rise after treatment, it took eight years to develop detectable metastatic cancer. After the metastatic cancer was found, the patients lived on average another five years.

Not all men with recurrent prostate cancer will follow this precise pattern, but this significant study established that recurrent prostate cancer tends to grow slowly in most men who initially had early stage, favorable grade disease and not every patient will need immediate intervention.

Symptoms of Recurrence

Will I have symptoms if my prostate cancer has returned?

No, probably not, if you are monitored with PSA tests. The first sign of cancer recurrence almost always is a rising PSA. Occasionally, a patient will recur with metastatic disease to the bone, lymph nodes, or other organs. Patients may have symptoms such as bone pain or have no symptoms at all. But symptoms such as bone pain as the first sign of recurrence are very unusual today. It was fairly common 20 years ago because we didn't have the PSA blood test. Now we typically know the prostate cancer is coming back because of the PSA rise. An increase in the PSA nearly always precedes a clinical recurrence—that is, the development of symptoms—by many years. It's unusual today for a prostate cancer patient who's been getting regular follow-up care to suddenly develop back or pelvic pain from undetected recurrent prostate cancer as the first sign of recurrence.

What tests will I have if my doctor thinks it's recurrent prostate cancer?

A patient will undergo a series of tests to find out where the cancer has spread. These tests may include a digital rectal exam (DRE), transrectal ultrasound, prostate biopsy, seminal vesicle biopsies, a bone scan, a CT scan, an MRI scan, or perhaps a ProstaScint scan.

Treatment Choices

What treatments are available if the cancer returns?

The treatments for recurrence are the same used for primary therapy: watchful waiting, surgery or cryosurgery, external beam radiation, seed implants, hormones, or investigational drugs in a clinical trial. If the PSA is rising without evidence of spread to bones or other sites, chemotherapy is generally used only in clinical trials.

Watchful Waiting

It's not uncommon for physicians to suggest watchful waiting in some cases of recurrence. Here's why: let's assume a 70-year-old man was treated with brachytherapy for early stage prostate cancer. Nine years later, his PSA starts to creep up. He's now 79 years old, has no symptoms, and is feeling well. Chances are high that he could go many years before developing any sign of cancer. Watchful waiting (with periodic monitoring, of course) is perfectly reasonable because the recurrent cancer may never become a problem in this man's life. Since patients can experience considerable side effects due to the treatments for recurrent prostate cancer, delaying therapy can be an attractive option.

Surgery Failure

Following a failed radical prostatectomy, salvage radiation is often given if the PSA is rising but there's no sign of distant spread. The salvage radiation dose is often lower than what's given as a first-line treatment and results are best if the PSA is less than 1 ng/mL. It is a noninvasive treatment that offers a reasonable success rate, especially if the PSA is under 1 ng/mL when the treatment is started. It has a low risk of permanent side effects.

External Beam Failure

Patients with local recurrence may be treated with a salvage seed implant, but the implant should be done with caution and only by a brachytherapist who is experienced in this situation. There is a high risk of incontinence, and other problems can occur when using more radiation on a prostate that's already been irradiated.

Performing a radical prostatectomy after any radiation is tricky and risky. Radiation causes some scarring of the prostate tissue and the surrounding tissue, which can make prostate removal difficult. The surgery can be done, but it takes an extreme amount of skill and experience. Sometimes both the prostate and the bladder must be removed. The risk of incontinence and erectile dysfunction is high. Also, radiated tissue is extremely slow to heal. We advise patients to seek an experienced surgeon in salvage prostatectomy if this option is considered.

Seed Failure

A second implant can be done but is usually not advised because it may cause serious complications, particularly incontinence and a narrowing of the urethra.

Retreatment with external beam radiation is not advised. The seeds have already emitted the highest tolerable radiation dose to the surrounding tissues; since the cancer cells survived such a high dose of radiation, any additional radiation probably would not kill the remaining cancer and might only serve to cause additional long-term complications.

Surgery may be considered in this situation. It is risky and rarely performed, but is perhaps slightly easier than in patients who had prior external beam radiation. This type of salvage surgery should only be performed by experienced surgeons.

Some men undergo cryosurgery after failed radiation, but there are little long-term data about its success as a salvage treatment. One main reason it's being used to treat recurrent prostate cancer is because it's less invasive than a radical prostatectomy. However, side effects may include incontinence, urinary retention, fistula formation, rectal pain, urinary infection, swelling in the area of the scrotum, blood in the urine, and an extremely high rate of erectile dysfunction. Like salvage surgery, cryosurgery should only be performed by doctors who have experience in this situation.

Hormonal Therapy

Hormonal therapy is one of the best treatments we have for recurrent prostate cancer. Hormone therapy treats prostate cancer recurrence regardless of whether it's a local or distant recurrence, whereas surgery, radiation, and cryosurgery are only used for local recurrence.

Hormonal manipulation is not curative but the vast majority of patients respond well for a period of time, usually years. That said, however, there is debate in the medical community about when to start hormone therapy after the PSA starts to rise. Hormones may be used early after recurrence. But for many men, no therapy may be the best choice. Men should be monitored with frequent PSA tests, physical exams, and periodic bone scans.

Chemotherapy

Hormonal therapy controls prostate cancer by depriving the cells of testosterone and other androgens. At some point, though, hormonal therapy may no longer be effective because some of the cancer cells were not originally responsive to hormones or they later became resistant to hormone treatment. If you have been on hormone treatments, the PSA may not necessarily tell the whole story. In other words, a person on hormonal treatment for a long time could be diagnosed with bone metastases and still have a low PSA. In any event, when hormonal treatments are no longer effective, it's time to consider chemotherapy.

Chemotherapy is used most often when hormonal treatments have failed and the cancer cells no longer respond to hormones. In recent years, it's been used earlier in patients to prevent the advancement of disease. Despite the fact that chemotherapy has not yet been shown to extend life expectancy in prostate cancer patients, many patients have had dramatic responses to chemotherapy and some individuals have definitely had their lives extended with chemotherapy.

Chemotherapy is injected directly into a vein or swallowed as a pill. The patient then goes into a short recovery period for a few days or weeks, and then gets another dose. The duration of treatment varies, depending on the drugs. Sometimes the medications are used alone, sometimes in combination. A few of the more common chemotherapy drugs used in prostate cancer are docetaxel (Taxotere), doxorubicin (Adriamycin), estramustine phosphate (Emcyt), etoposide (Vepsid), mitoxantrone (Novantrone), paclitaxel (Taxol), and vinblastine (Velban). The combination of mitoxantrone and prednisone is often used in patients with hormone-resistant prostate cancer who are also in pain. The taxanes (docetaxel or paclitaxel) are used alone or in combination with estramustine or other agents such as calcitriol.

Chemotherapy drugs kill cells as they divide, and fast-growing cancer cells are more susceptible to these drugs than normal cells. Some other fast-growing cells—hair follicles, the lining of the gastrointestinal tract, and bone marrow—may also be temporarily affected by the chemotherapy. Although these noncancerous cells may be damaged by the therapy, the body will restore them after the chemotherapy is stopped. Specific side effects will depend on the type, amount, and duration of the drugs. Medication can control some of the side effects, including nausea and vomiting. The most commonly reported temporary side effects include:

- Bleeding or bruising from minor injuries
- Diarrhea
- Fatigue related to anemia
- Hair loss
- Loss of appetite

- Mouth sores
- Nausea and vomiting
- Risk of infection

Bisphosphonates

These are drugs that diminish the bone-destroying activity caused by cancer in the bone. Zoledronic acid (Zometa) may be used with chemotherapy or other hormonal treatments. It has been shown to delay and minimize the development of skeletal complications in men who have early hormone-refractory prostate cancer with bone metastases.

Should I be in a clinical trial?

We sometimes suggest that our patients consider participating in a clinical trial. Participation is completely voluntary, of course. These studies can help discover new ways to improve prostate cancer care and treatment. Clinical trials help answer questions about prevention, diagnosis, and treatment of prostate cancer. There are multiple places to search for information about clinical trials. One of the best places to start is the National Cancer Institute (NCI). Its PDQ database contains information about trials conducted around the country as well as those conducted by the NCI. These include innovative surgical therapy, radiation therapy, chemotherapy trials, biologic therapy, gene therapy, or vaccine trials. (See Appendix B for NCI contact information.) Many institutions also have their own clinical trials website that patients can access via the Internet.

What about the last stages of prostate cancer? Is there anything doctors can do?

Sometimes, after everything has been tried, the cancer still advances. The treatments left are those to minimize bone pain or other discomfort that may come with late stage prostate cancer. This type of care is called palliative care, and there are many successful strategies to help during this time.

Investigational Therapies for Prostate Cancer

New drugs and treatments to fight prostate cancer are under constant development. Here's a brief rundown of some of the more promising investigational treatments:

Immune Therapy

Several treatments looking at whether the body's own immune system can fight the prostate cancer are now being explored.

- Dendritic cells—which are from the immune system—are taken from the patient's blood, treated in the lab to generate a response to fight prostate cancer, and injected back into the patient.
- Anti-CTLA-4 is an antibody that stimulates T-cells, which are cells from the immune system that can fight prostate cancer.
- Vaccine trials examine whether specific substances elicit an immune response to kill prostate cancer cells.

There are also investigations into drugs that block growth factors—these are the proteins that cause tumor cells to divide and grow. Science is also examining whether drugs that impede the tumor's ability to generate a network of blood vessels will kill the tumor. It's thought that starving the tumor will stop it from growing.

These are only a few of the many new therapies under development, with many more on the horizon.

Radioisotopes

Strontium-89 and samarium-153 are isotopes that emit a short, low-dose radiation and can be used to alleviate bone pain. These isotopes are injected by a radiation oncologist or diagnostic radiologist into a vein. They concentrate in those areas of the bone that contain cancer and deliver the radiation dose exactly where it is needed. This results in cancer cell death, decreases bone pain, and lessens the need for medications. The response rate is about 80 percent and the side effects are minimal. It can delay the appearance of other painful bone metastases.

Radiation

One of the most useful treatments to relieve bone pain is external beam radiation. A short course of radiation, usually about two to four weeks to the specific area of pain, can bring about dramatic relief and strengthen the bone, prevent fracture, and prevent or treat spinal cord injury. This can be very important to preserve a high quality of life and keep patients independent and at home.

Hospice Care

For patients in the final days, weeks, or months of life, hospice care can provide an important source of dignity, comfort, and peace. Hospice care involves health professionals and volunteers who give medical, emotional, psychological, and spiritual support. An important physical aspect of hospice care is pain control. Hospice care can take place at home, in hospice facilities or hospitals, or in skilled nursing centers.

A Final Thought

It is important to realize that treatments for recurrent disease are constantly improving and are patient-specific. Patients with recurrent prostate cancer can live productive and useful lives for many years. If the cancer recurs, it is important that a physician carefully follow its course and intervene with the right treatments at the right times. The vast majority of patients respond well to these therapies, and today the side effects are being managed better, making a significant difference in the quality of life.

Part III

OTHER IMPORTANT CONSIDERATIONS

12

What Should I Ask My Doctor?

Jeff M. Michalski, M.D.; John C. Blasko, M.D.

WHEN PATIENTS ARE sitting in our offices to discuss treatment options, we expect a lot of questions. We know that you probably have a list of your own questions to ask your physicians, but we'd like to pose a few for you to add to your list.

We're approaching this a bit differently than other books, however. There are a few questions that almost all brachytherapists are asked. For these questions, we're going to provide what we think are the kinds of answers you want to find. You'll also notice that during the course of giving our answer, we pose even *more* questions. These additional queries are meant to get you thinking in new ways and end up asking the most important questions to help you understand the skill level of your physicians.

We focus on brachytherapy, but many of these questions can be adapted for use with other specialists. At the end of this chapter, we also offer a list of additional questions you could add to your list.

How many patients have you treated with brachytherapy?
This is a frequent question, and the patient who's asking this is really asking about the physician's level of experience. It's fine to ask how many seed

procedures a brachytherapist has done during his or her career, but the answer reveals only part of the picture.

Besides asking about the number of seed implants, we encourage you to ask follow-up questions. Inquire about the approximate number of implants the physician performs each month. The frequency of implants being done each month can be an indicator of the brachytherapist's medical reputation. For example, if the doctor you're talking to has done 50 seed implants in the last two or three months then this clearly tells you that other doctors are comfortable referring patients to this individual.

There's another reason to ask about the number of monthly implants. This procedure has a steep learning curve. If a physician performs one a month, there's little chance to climb the curve.

We also encourage patients to ask about the physician's overall medical training. Questions can run along the lines of, "What is your training in brachytherapy? Was prostate brachytherapy part of your residency program? Was your residency or training at a strong academic institution or center that does a large number of seed implants?"

In short, asking how many seed implants a doctor has performed can be an indicator of ability. But, there's more that matters than simply the number of brachytherapy cases.

Where did you receive your training in prostate brachytherapy?

There are different ways a doctor can be trained to do seed implants. Today, a lot of residency training programs train doctors how to do seed implants as part of the overall radiation therapy program. For those physicians who didn't get it during their residency, a number of courses are offered by expert brachytherapists. Physicians tend to use these as an introduction to the procedure and go on to take other courses through professional societies, watch the technique of other physicians in the operating room, or have brachytherapy specialists come and watch or help them do it. You might want to ask if your physician is involved in the teaching or training of other physicians to do the procedure. This reflects an ability and higher level of knowledge than other practitioners.

What's your success rate in brachytherapy?

There are a couple of different ways to define success. If a brachytherapist does routine quality assurance he or she can tell you, for instance, that 90 percent or 95 percent of the time the radiation doses fall within published guidelines. That's one way to look at success.

The more difficult definition of success is the number of patients who are alive and free of any sign of cancer five and 10 years after this physician or group of physicians started doing the implants. There are a small number of centers in the United States that have published five-year results, and even fewer that have published ten-year results with current, modern techniques. Does this mean that you have to go to those centers to get the best care? No, we don't think so. However, it's appropriate to ask, "Do you examine your clinical outcomes?"

An even more important question for the patient who's seeing a brachytherapist who has done this procedure for 5 or 10 years is, "Is there anything about your experience that you feel is outside of the expected results, or are you seeing results comparable to previously published results?"

What seed would you recommend and why?

Patients used to ask this a lot, but we're getting this question less and less frequently. Occasionally, a patient will come with a brochure or they'll have found something on the Internet and ask about a particular seed. Some physicians prefer one seed over another, but in truth there's enough evidence today to say that they're equivalent with respect to outcome.

How many seeds will you order? What determines the number of seeds used?

The study of the size of the prostate (the volume study) helps determine the number of seeds. A question that would net you more information would be, "What determines the number of seeds you use?" Some brachytherapists use many seeds of very low activity. Others use fewer seeds of higher activity. The decision to use one versus the other will depend on the doctor's background, training, and experience. There's a balance between experience, volume of gland, and activity of seeds, so all of that will come into play in determining the number of seeds to be implanted.

Do you give external beam radiation to every patient?

We know that combining external beam with a seed implant carries a greater risk of side effects and increases the cost of treatment. To treat every patient who gets a seed implant with external beam therapy is probably not necessary. A boost of external beam radiation should be reserved for seed patients who need it—those who have a higher-risk cancer.

If external beam therapy is medically necessary, patients usually have about 25 sessions. We encourage you find out exactly what area will be treated with the external radiation. In the older, more traditional way, some doctors will treat the whole pelvic area with the added radiation—prostate, seminal vesicles, and regional lymph nodes. Other physicians who use more modern techniques will treat just the prostate and the seminal vesicles. But if the risk of lymph node involvement is significant, even modern centers may use whole pelvic radiation in selected patients.

Some physicians will use 3D conformal radiation therapy to minimize the volume of the bladder and rectum from receiving the same dose of radiation as the prostate and immediately adjacent tissues. This may reduce side effects from the external beam radiation therapy. A newer form of radiation therapy, intensity modulated radiation therapy (IMRT), is probably not necessary when combining external radiation therapy with a seed implant but neither is it harmful. When a patient is getting high doses of external radiation therapy alone for his cancer, IMRT offers some advantages. However, as part of the treatment for a patient who is getting a seed implant, IMRT unnecessarily contributes greater complexity and cost for the relatively modest doses of radiation therapy used with combination therapy.

How many of your patients require a catheter?

This is an important question. Patients who have a seed implant need to understand that they *might* need a catheter for a while. Here's why. There are two phases of prostate irritation after implant. There's the immediate swelling that comes from the trauma of the needles. Then in a few weeks when the radiation from the seeds is having its maximum effect on the prostate, the gland can be inflamed and swollen and the urethra can become incapable of passing urine. This is the higher-risk time for needing a catheter.

When you ask, "How many of your patients require a catheter?" the ideal answer is that less than one in 10 patients will need a catheter for any length of time. If the doctor says, "One-third of my patients need a catheter several weeks after the implant," that raises a red flag. It could indicate that high-risk patients are being selected—perhaps their prostates are large or there was a high degree of urinary symptoms before the implant. It may also suggest something about the implant technique. Maybe the doctor is not skilled in placing the needles and needed many tries to get the needle in the right spot, causing more trauma. Be sure to ask about the details.

Can I speak to some of your patients?

This is a fine question to ask the doctor. But not all patients are willing to talk to other patients because they want to keep their privacy. Also, with new federal privacy laws protecting a patient's health care information, it is more difficult now to get this kind of permission.

Some physicians keep a list of patients who are willing to be contacted, while other doctors will contact a more recent patient to see if he's willing to take a call. Don't be put off if the doctor needs a few days to find out if a patient wants to talk to you. Not all physicians keep a list because those lists are often hard to maintain.

Do you participate in clinical trials?

Not every patient needs to be in a clinical trial; however, clinical trials are critical to advancing knowledge about prostate cancer treatment.

To illustrate our point, let's talk about the importance of clinical trials in treating another kind of cancer. Twenty years ago, women were undergoing mastectomies every time they were diagnosed with a malignant breast cancer. Nearly every woman lost her breast as a result of the diagnosis of breast cancer. If it weren't for courageous women participating in a clinical trial, we would still be doing mastectomies on most of these patients. Today, mastectomy is done with far less frequency than lumpectomy and radiation. It's only because of trials that showed lumpectomy plus radiation is at least as effective as mastectomy that we've been able to answer many important questions.

If you're in your doctor's office discussing whether or not to enroll in a randomized trial comparing surgery to seeds,[15] for instance, you might think to yourself, "Why would I allow a computer to determine my treatment when I want my physician to tell me what's best?" That's the problem. We don't know what's best. We know that brachytherapy is a good treatment. We also know that surgery is a good treatment. But they may have different consequences, different side effects, and the like.

By being in a trial, you'll be contributing to the understanding of cancer so that 10 years from now patients sitting in their doctors' offices will have better information. Fifty years from now when your grandsons are in a similar office having a similar conversation about what kind of prostate cancer treatment to have, they'll be better able to choose because of what you did by enrolling in this kind of randomized trial.

Besides asking whether the physician participates in clinical trials, ask which trials are available to you, what questions are the trials asking, and why your physician would recommend it for you. But remember, being in a trial is always optional. No one should make you feel that you must participate.

Other Questions to Consider Asking

- What tests will I undergo and when will I get the results?
- Do I call to get the results of the tests, or does someone from your office call me?
- Who do I contact to get copies of my tests and records?
- What is my PSA? What is my Gleason score? What stage is my cancer?
- What treatment do you recommend and why?
- What treatment options do I have?
- If you recommend surgery, is nerve-sparing surgery possible?
- If you recommend external beam radiation therapy, what kind of external beam do you recommend? Why?
- If you recommend seed implants, will they be used alone or with another therapy? Why or why not?
- How many patients have you treated with brachytherapy? What is your training in brachytherapy?
- What's your success rate in brachytherapy?
- How long will my entire treatment last?
- What kind of PSA results can I expect with this treatment?
- Who will do the follow-up? Who am I going to call if I have trouble after treatment?
- How many of your patients require a catheter and for how long?
- Can I talk with some of your other patients?
- What are the side effects of the treatment you recommend, and when might they occur?

- In your hands, what are the rates of incontinence, erectile dysfunction, and bowel problems with the kind of treatment you are recommending?
- What is your definition of incontinence?
- How long will the side effects last?
- What treatments are available to manage the side effects? How costly are these treatments?
- Who do I call if I'm having acute problems?
- Are there medications or activities I should avoid following treatment?
- Do I need to be on a special diet? Can I continue to take my vitamins? Can I speak to a dietician while I am receiving treatment?
- Do you participate in clinical trials? Are there any current trials being done that I would qualify for, given my grade and stage of prostate cancer?
- Can you recommend local support groups for me? What about a support group for my spouse?
- Is there a social worker or therapist that I can talk to at this hospital if my significant other or I need support?

13

How Do I Find the Best Doctor for Brachytherapy?

Gregory S. Merrick, M.D.; Bradley R. Prestidge, M.D.;
Peter D. Grimm, D.O.

AFTER YOU'VE DECIDED to undergo brachytherapy your next questions may be, "Where should I have my therapy done? Should I go to a large center or can it be performed in my community hospital?" There are many skilled brachytherapists in community settings as well as at large centers. In fact, the physician in your neighborhood could be as skilled, if not more so, than the brachytherapist practicing in the regional facility. But how can you determine which doctor has the best patient outcomes?

In these next few pages, we discuss general quality assurance (QA) activities that brachytherapists undertake. Our goal is to help you understand how QA has made brachytherapy one of the safest, most convenient, and successful treatments for the right prostate cancer patient, and how you are the beneficiary of all the behind-the-scenes meetings and analysis that goes into a solid QA program.

What exactly is brachytherapy QA?
The essence of QA is to verify that the team is properly performing the procedure and is doing it to the best of its ability. Quality assurance means

engaging in a systematic review of prostate implants with medical team members including nurses, dosimetrists, physicists, and, of course, physicians. The team reviews statistics such as radiation dose and how it's distributed throughout the prostate (this is called dosimetry).

Quality assurance meetings are also a venue to discuss problems and figure out solutions. For instance, the team can confer about what to do in cases with less-than-ideal dosimetry. Other activities include discussing medical papers and brachytherapy articles to help all team members keep up with the latest brachytherapy advancements.

What does a prostate brachytherapy QA program measure?

There are several yardsticks, but the most common way of assessing the quality of the implant is to evaluate the postoperative dosimetry. This involves a computer calculation resulting in a series of images showing the actual radiation dose received by the prostate, urethra, bladder, and rectum. This result is then compared to the planned dose. Although there is no universal agreement as to the exact radiation doses that need to be delivered, there are some general guidelines that exist in the medical literature.

A QA program can also monitor prostate specific antigen (PSA) control, urinary, rectal, and sexual function. It takes at least five years to accumulate these kinds of long-term statistics. Centers of excellence do tend to have such data, but these centers are relatively few and far between.

How does a physician check the quality of a seed implant?

The most common way to check the quality of a seed implant is by performing a CT scan following the implant. This is usually done anytime from the day of the implant to as long as 30 days afterward. This dose analysis is then compared to the original prescription. This allows the physician to evaluate his or her performance. Although there is some controversy about the ideal dose delivery criteria that should be achieved, there are general guidelines in existence that most physicians accept.

There are some physicians who either do not perform any kind of analysis of implant quality following the implant or simply use x-rays of the seeds to calculate a very crude form of dosimetry. Neither of these approaches are considered acceptable by modern standards. An important question to ask your physician is whether or not CT-based, postimplant dosimetry is performed as part of a QA program.

Does the number of cases a center performs indicate quality?

It's generally true that the more times a person performs a task, the better he or she is at it. This is a well-proven concept in many areas of medicine—notably cardiovascular surgery and radical prostatectomy—and it's becoming evident in brachytherapy.

To specifically answer the question, we believe that, in general, a physician must perform at least 50 to 100 implants a year consistently to stay proficient. While volume of implants performed often correlates with good quality, exceptions exist. We are aware of many centers that do a small number of implants, do them consistently well, engage in quality assurance activities, and achieve excellent outcomes. Conversely, a center may be doing hundreds of cases a year, but if it fails to review dosimetry as well as complications regarding urinary, bowel, and sexual function in conjunction with PSA data, a true gauge of how patients are faring cannot be obtained.

Does anyone periodically review how doctors do implants?

Brachytherapy techniques are undergoing subtle changes all of the time, which is why there is no standard technique for performing an implant. Although there is no single way of doing an implant, many of the techniques work very well. That's another reason why QA is so important. The postimplant assessment lets doctors measure whether a technique is working or not, particularly if the complication and cancer control rates are tracked. The QA process collects irrefutable evidence that answers questions such as, "What is the consistency of the implant technique? Are the implants consistently done well?"

What are the criteria for a good implant?

It's well established that getting the correct dose is important in achieving a cure. It's also known that complication rates appear related to implant technique—radiation doses that are too high have resulted in increased urinary problems, erectile dysfunction, rectal bleeding, and other complications. That's why preplanning is important—whether it's done days before the procedure or right in the operating room—as well as postimplant assessment to document the radiation distribution.

There is currently a large body of data regarding radiation dose and biochemical and quality of life outcomes, but the minimum and maximum radiation recommendations for the greatest chance of cure with the fewest side effects have not been completely documented. The American Brachytherapy Society (ABS) recommends that doctors collect several dosimetry measurements for each implant; this additional data may be used to "tweak" the current commonly accepted dose parameters.

What can be done if the implant is poor?

If the postoperative dosimetry suggests the dose distribution is less than ideal to control the cancer, watchful waiting could be appropriate even if the implant is suboptimal; the radiation dose may be in just the right regions and in just the right strength to defeat the cancer. Another option is a second implant covering the specific areas where the radiation is too low. Other choices may include high-dose rate (HDR) temporary implantation or external beam radiation.

Radical prostatectomy is something else to consider. Because brachytherapy patients elected an implant in the first place, they're unlikely to be excited about the idea of radical surgery the second time around. Complicating this choice is the technical difficulty of removing a prostate following radiation treatment. Most communities do not have urologic surgeons with this expertise. This patient would likely be asked to travel to a major treatment center to be treated by a surgeon who's skilled in removing prostates after radiotherapy has been done.

I contacted the companies that make brachytherapy seeds and asked for a physician recommendation. Is it advisable to take this recommendation?

Speaking with the companies that make the seeds is one way to arrive at a potential list of physicians.[16] Keep in mind, though, that companies refer patients to physicians who use their seeds, and these firms are in no position to evaluate the quality of the physician. Ask the company what criteria it uses for including the doctor on its list. Also, when you meet with a physician suggested by a seed company, be sure to ask him or her all of the questions you would ask other brachytherapists.

What organizations credential brachytherapy centers?

Credentialing means that an outside body, such as a medical society or governmental entity, sets the minimum standard of performance for a medical facility or program. If the medical program meets or exceeds these agreed upon standards, then it's considered "credentialed."

Regarding prostate seed implants, no brachytherapy-related society has a formal credentialing process yet. But the Radiation Therapy Oncology Group (RTOG), an organization of 250 centers in the United States and Canada engaging in radiation therapy research, will collect national data in an effort to scientifically define what constitutes a good or an unacceptable implant. By correlating implant quality to patient outcomes, it should be possible to set minimum standards that will serve as a guideline to practicing brachytherapists throughout the country. With the recent initiation of the first randomized, prospective prostate brachytherapy trial by the RTOG, we hope that these standards will be formulated in the near future.

Similarly, the University of Washington and the Schiffler Cancer Center are currently completing two large prospective randomized trials examining the influence of isotope, supplemental external beam radiation, and multiple dosimetric parameters on both biochemical outcome and quality of life measures. More than 1,200 patients are involved in these studies, and the results should be available in a few years.

Are there independent companies or agents that verify brachytherapy centers?

Yes. If facilities desire help for QA activities outside of what they do themselves or through their own hospitals, they can turn to independent quality assurance firms.[17] These companies, usually run by physicians who are recognized as experts by their peers, provide many services—helping plan the number and location of seeds before implant, scrutinizing the implant afterward to determine if the dose matches the plan, and suggesting improvements to the entire team.

What should I do if my brachytherapist doesn't do QA?

It is important that patients work with a brachytherapist who is committed to performing high-quality implants with a dedicated and intensive follow-up protocol, both for data collection and to determine the long-term implications of prostate seed implantation on potential cure and quality of life outcomes including urinary, bowel, and sexual function. If the brachytherapist is not involved in such endeavors, additional consultation would appear prudent.

APPENDIX A

The Bottom Line

BELOW IS A rundown of the advantages of each of the major treatments discussed in this book.

Advantages of Watchful Waiting

- No side effects, initially
- Many men die of other causes before they die of prostate cancer

Advantages of Surgery

- Modern-era, 10-year outcomes data are published
- Stage II patients in the low- and intermediate-risk groups are good candidates
- Advantageous for patients with significant obstructive urinary symptoms because surgery treats both the obstructive symptoms and the cancer
- Low risk of bowel toxicity
- Salvage radiation therapy can help a minority of surgical failures

Advantages of External Beam Radiation Therapy (specifically 3D-CRT)

- Noninvasive
- Five-year results in low-risk patients are comparable to the five-year surgical and seed results
- Wide range of patients are candidates
- Low risk of incontinence
- Low risk of urinary retention

Advantages of Permanent Prostate Seed Implantation

- Modern-era, 10-year outcome data are published
- No other treatment has better long-term disease control rates
- Stage II patients in the low-, intermediate-, and high-risk groups are good candidates
- Single outpatient treatment
- Low risk of incontinence
- Low risk of erectile dysfunction
- Only need a few days off work
- Posttreatment quality assessment allows brachytherapists to "enhance" the occasional suboptimal implant

Advantages of Hormonal Therapy

- Low risk of bowel and bladder side effects
- Most men enjoy a temporary remission of their disease
- Noninvasive

APPENDIX B

Prostate Cancer Resources

Seattle Prostate Institute
1101 Madison Street, Suite 1101
Seattle, WA 98104
www.seattleprostate.com
info@seattleprostate.com

What would you add to this book? Is there a question you have that wasn't asked? We invite you to send us questions for possible inclusion in future editions of *The Prostate Cancer Treatment Book*. Please send us your thoughts via E-mail or regular mail (addresses above).

Books

ABC's of Advanced Prostate Cancer
Mark A. Moyad, M.P.H., and Kenneth J. Pienta, M.D. Chelsea, MI:
Sleeping Bear Press, 2000.

ABC's of Nutrition and Supplements for Prostate Cancer
Mark A. Moyad, M.P.H. Chelsea, MI: Sleeping Bear Press, 2000.

ABC's of Prostate Cancer: The Book That Could Save Your Life
Joseph E. Oesterling, M.D., and Mark A. Moyad, M.P.H. Lanham, MD:
Madison Books, 1997.

The American Cancer Society: Prostate Cancer: What Every Man and His Family Needs to Know (Revised Edition)
David G. Bostwick, M.D., et al. New York: Villard Books, 1999.

Getting the Best From Your Doctor : An Insider's Guide to the Health Care You Deserve
Alan N. Swartz, M.D., et al. Minneapolis, MN: Chronimed Publishing, 1998.

Hit Below the Belt: Facing Up to Prostate Cancer
F. Ralph Berberich, M.D., Berkeley, CA: Celestial Arts, 2001.

How I Survived Prostate Cancer . . . and So Can You
James Lewis and Roy Berger. Westbury, NY: Health Education Literary Publishers, 1994.

Living with Prostate Cancer: One Man's Story: What Everyone Should Know
Audrey Currie Newton. Toronto: McClelland & Stewart, 1996.

Man to Man: Surviving Prostate Cancer
Michael Korda. New York: Random House, 1996; Vintage Books, 1997.

Me Too: A Doctor Survives Prostate Cancer
James E. Payne. Waco, TX: WRS Publishing, 1995.

Men, Women, and Prostate Cancer: A Medical and Psychological Guide for Women and the Men They Love (Second Edition)
Barbara Rubin Wainrib, et al. Oakland, CA: New Harbinger, 2000.

New Guidelines for Surviving Prostate Cancer
James Lewis, Jr., M.D., and E. Roy Berger, M.D. Westbury, NY: Health Education Literary Publishers, 1997.

100 Questions and Answers About Prostate Cancer
Pamela Ellsworth, M.D., et al. Sudbury, MA: Jones and Bartlett Publishers, 2002.

The Patient's Guide to Prostate Cancer: An Expert's Successful Treatment Strategies and Options
Marc Garnick, M.D. New York: Penguin Books, 1996.

A Primer on Prostate Cancer: The Empowered Patient's Guide
Stephen Strum, M.D., and Donna Pogliano. Hollywood, FL: Life
  Extension Foundation, 2002.

Prostate Cancer: A Non-Surgical Perspective
Kent Wallner, M.D. Seattle, WA: SmartMedicine Press, 2000.

*The Prostate Cancer Answer Book: An Unbiased Guide to
  Treatment Choices*
Marion E. Morra, et al. New York: Avon Books, 1996.

Prostate Cancer: Detection and Cure
A. M. Durrani, M.D. Burnet, TX: Swan Publishing, 1997.

Prostate Cancer: A Doctor's Personal Triumph
Saralee Fine and Robert Fine, M.D. Forest Dale, VT: Paul S.
  Eriksson Publishers, 1999.

*Prostate Cancer: A Family Guide to Diagnosis, Treatment
  and Survival*
Sheldon Marks, M.D. Cambridge, MA: Perseus
  Publishing, 1999.

*Prostate Cancer: Overcoming Denial with Action: A Guide to
  Screening, Treatment and Healing*
Allen E. Salowe, et al. New York: St. Martin's Press, 1998.

*The Prostate Cancer Sourcebook: How to Make Informed
  Treatment Choices*
Marcus Loo, M.D., and Marian Betancourt. New York: John Wiley
  & Sons, 1998.

Prostate Cancer: A Survivor's Guide
Donald F. Kaltenbach, et al. New Port Richey, FL: Seneca House
  Press, 1996.

*Prostate Cancer: Treatment and Recovery: Confronting the Emotional
  and Physical Challenges*
Richard Y. Handy. Amherst, NY: Prometheus Books, 1996.

*A Revolutionary Approach to Prostate Cancer: Alternatives to Standard
   Treatment Options: Doctors and Survivors Share Their Knowledge*
Aubrey Pilgrim and Stephen M. Auerbach. New York: Sterling House
   Publishers, 1998.

Seeds of Hope: A Physician's Personal Triumph over Prostate Cancer
Michael A. Dorso, M.D. Battle Creek, MI: Acorn Publishing, 2000.

SmartMedicine: How to Cut Medical Costs and Cure Cancer
Kent Wallner, M.D. Seattle, WA: SmartMedicine Press, 2000.

What Can I Do? My Husband Has Prostate Cancer
Beverly Farmer. Battle Ground, WA: Pathfinder Press, 1995

Medical Literature

Assistance with obtaining copies of these publications may be available
through the medical library of your local hospital or directly from the rel-
evant organizations.

American Cancer Society. *Sexuality & Cancer: For the Man Who Has
   Cancer and His Partner*, October 1995.
———. *Prostate Cancer: Treatment Guidelines for Patients*, June 1999.
Beyer, D., et al. "Biochemical disease-free survival following iodine-125
   prostate implantation," 1997, *International Journal of Radiation Oncology
   Biology Physics* 37: 359–363.
Blasko, J. "Brachytherapy," 2000, *Urology* 55: 306–308.
———. "The future of prostate brachytherapy," 2001, *Journal of
   Brachytherapy International* 17: 255–257.
Blasko, J., et al. "Brachytherapy for carcinoma of the prostate: techniques,
   patient selection, and clinical outcomes," 2002, *Seminars in Radiation
   Oncology* 12(1): 81–94.
———. "Palladium-103 brachytherapy for prostate carcinoma," 2000,
   International Journal of Radiation Oncology Biology Physics 46(4):
   839–850.
———. "The role of external beam radiotherapy with I-125/Pd-103
   brachytherapy for prostate carcinoma," 2000, *Radiotherapy & Oncology*
   57(3): 273–78.

Davis, B. J., et al. "Adjuvant external radiation therapy following radical prostatectomy for node-negative prostate cancer," 2003, *Current Opinion in Urology* 13(2): 117–122.

———. "The radial distance of extraprostatic extension of prostate cancer: implications for prostate brachytherapy," 1999, *Cancer* 85: 2630–37.

———. "Treatment of extraprostatic cancer in clinically organ confined prostate cancer by permanent interstitial brachytherapy: Is extraprostatic seed placement necessary?" 2000, *Techniques in Urology* 6: 70–77.

Dattoli, M., et al. "Pd-103 brachytherapy and external beam irradiation for clinically localized high risk prostatic carcinoma," 1996, *International Journal of Radiation Oncology Biology Physics* 35: 875–879.

Friedrich, M. J. "Issues in prostate cancer screening," 1999, *Journal of the American Medical Association* 281(17): 1573.

Grimm, P. "10-year biochemical (prostate-specific antigen) control of prostate cancer with 125-i brachytherapy," 2001, *International Journal of Radiation Oncology Biology Physics* 51: 31–40.

Grimm, P., et al. "Clinical selection issues for permanent seed prostate brachytherapy," 2001, *Journal of Brachytherapy International* 17: 143–152.

———. "Transperineal ultrasound guided I-125/Pd-103 brachytherapy for early stage prostate cancer: update on clinical experience at seven years," (abstract), 1997, *International Journal of Radiation Oncology Biology Physics* 39 (Suppl.): 1008.

Henderson, C. "Brachytherapy produced high cure rate for 'low risk' prostate cancer," *Cancer Weekly*, Nov. 15, 1999.

Leibovich, B. C., et al. "Proximity of prostate cancer to the urethra: implications for minimally invasive ablative therapies," 2000, *Urology* 56(5): 726–729.

Marwick, C. "ACS sets blueprint for action against prostate cancer in African-Americans," 1998, *Journal of the American Medical Association* 279(6): 418.

Merrick, G., et al. "Five-year biochemical outcome following permanent interstitial brachytherapy for clinical T1-T3 prostate cancer," 2001, *International Journal of Radiation Oncology Biology Physics* 51(1): 41–48.

———. "Short-term sexual function after prostate brachytherapy," 2001, *International Journal of Cancer* 96(5): 313–319.

Mettlin, C., et al. "The national cancer database report on increased use of brachytherapy for the treatment of patients with prostate carcinoma in the U.S.," 1999, *Cancer* 86(9): 1877.

National Cancer Institute, *What You Need to Know About Prostate Cancer*, June 1996.

Pisansky, T. M., et al. "The relevance of prostatectomy findings in brachytherapy selection for localized prostate cancer," 2002, *Cancer* 95: 513–519.

Pisansky, T. M., and B. J. Davis. "Predictive factors in localized prostate cancer: implications for radiotherapy and clinical trial design," 2000, *Seminars in Urologic Oncology* 18: 93–107.

Stanford, J., et al. "Urinary and sexual function after radical prostatectomy for clinically localized prostate cancer: the prostate cancer outcomes study," 2000, *Journal of the American Medical Association* 283(3): 254–262.

Stock, R., et al. "The effect of prognostic factors on therapeutic outcome following transperineal prostate brachytherapy," 1997, *Seminars in Surgical Oncology* 13: 454–460.

Sylvester, J. "Urethral visualization during transrectal ultrasound-guided interstitial implantation for early stage prostate cancer" in: Annual Meeting of the Radiological Society of North America, Chicago, IL, 1998.

Sylvester, J., et al. "Brachytherapy as monotherapy," In: *Prostate Cancer: Principles and Practice*, pp. 336–357, P. Kantoff, P. C. Carroll, A. V. D'Amico, eds. Philadelphia: Lippincot Williams & Wilkins, 2001.

———. "Impact of short-course androgen ablation on the biochemical progression-free survival of high-risk prostate cancer patients managed with permanent brachytherapy," 2001, *Journal of Brachytherapy International* 17: 173–180.

———. "Interstitial implantation techniques in prostate cancer," 1997, *Journal of Surgical Oncology* 66: 65–75.

———. "Modern prostate brachytherapy," 2002, *Oncology Issues* 17: 34–39.

————. "125-Iodine/103-Palladium brachytherapy with or without neoadjuvant brachytherapy for early stage prostate cancer (abstract)," 2000, *International Journal of Radiation, Oncology, Biology, Physics* 48(3): 310.

————. "The role of androgen ablation in patients with biochemical or local failure after definitive radiation therapy: a survey of practice patterns of urologists and radiation oncologists in the United States," 2001, *Urology* 58 (Suppl 2A): 65–70.

————. "Short-course androgen ablation combined with external-beam radiation therapy and low-dose-rate permanent brachytherapy in early stage prostate cancer: a matched subset analysis" 2000, *Molecular Urology* 4(3): 155–160.

————. "Transperineal permanent brachytherapy for local recurrence following external beam radiation for early-stage prostate cancer," 2001, *Journal of Brachytherapy International* 17: 181–188.

Wallner, K., et al. "Tumor control and morbidity following transperineal iodine-125 implantation for Stage T1/T2 prostatic carcinoma," 1996, *Journal of Clinical Oncology* 14: 449–453.

Other Resources

Below is a partial list of the numerous public and private organizations that provide information and other services related to prostate cancer. This list should not be taken as a recommendation or endorsement. Each patient needs to carefully weigh the information found through these or any other organizations and thoroughly discuss any details with your own physician(s).

American Brachytherapy Society
12100 Sunset Hills Road, Suite 130
Reston, VA 20190
703-234-4078
www.americanbrachytherapy.org

The ABS is a nonprofit organization for medical professionals. Its website contains a section for patients who are considering brachytherapy as a treatment option.

American Cancer Society
1599 Clifton Road NE
Atlanta, GA 30329
800-ACS-2345 (800-227-2345)
www.cancer.org

The ACS is a nationwide, community-based health organization headquartered in Atlanta with thousands of local offices.

American Foundation for Urologic Disease
1128 N. Charles Street
Baltimore, MD 21201
410-468-1800
www.afud.org

This nonprofit organization provides education, support, research, and advocacy.

American Health Information Management Association
233 N. Michigan Avenue, Suite 2150
Chicago, IL 60601
312-233-1100
www.ahima.org

AHIMA is for health care information professionals, but its website contains information about how to get the most out of your health care records and what health information to keep in your records at home.

American Urological Association
1120 N. Charles Street
Baltimore, MD 21201
410-727-1100
www.auanet.org

This professional association is dedicated to the advancement of urologic patient care. It has an online patient information resource.

Canadian Cancer Society
10 Alcorn Avenue, Suite 200
Toronto, Ontario
Canada M4V 3B1
416-961-7223
www.cancer.ca

This terrific organization provides support and information.

CancerFacts
NexCura, Inc.
1725 Westlake Avenue N, Suite 300
Seattle, WA 98109
877-422-3228
www.cancerfacts.com

This site offers a variety of educational and resource information plus a unique Cancer Profiler, an interactive tool that uses published scientific information to provide patients with treatment-related reports based on their medical history, test results, and personal preferences.

CaP CURE
1250 Fourth Street, Suite 360
Santa Monica, CA 90401
800-757-CURE
www.capcure.org

Founded in 1993 by financier Michael Milken following his prostate cancer diagnosis, CaP CURE is a nonprofit organization dedicated to finding cures and controls of this disease.

The Circle
www.prostatepointers.org/circle

The Circle is a mailing list and website offering support for wives, families, friends, and significant others of men with prostate cancer.

Foundation for Informed Medical Decision Making

This organization offers a patient-advice video that deals with treatment options entitled "Is a PSA Test Right for You?" It can be purchased on the Internet at www.collaborativecare.net/psaindex.html.

Healthfinder
P.O. Box 1133
Washington, DC 20013
800-336-4797
www.healthfinder.gov

A service of the U.S. Department of Health and Human Services, this site leads to selected online publications, clearinghouses, databases, websites, support groups, and much more.

Hospice Education Institute
3 Unity Square
P.O. Box 98
Machiasport, ME 04655
800-331-1620
www.hospiceworld.org

This organization offers information and referrals on hospice programs around the country, and it provides regional seminars on hospice care throughout the United States.

Man to Man
c/o American Cancer Society
1599 Clifton Road NE
Atlanta, GA 30329
800-ACS-2345 (800-227-2345)
www.cancer.org

Established in cooperation with the American Cancer Society, this program offers a network of local support groups, in-person and telephone support, a newsletter, and other services. Some Man to Man meetings invite significant others to attend. For others, wives and partners may meet separately in groups called Side by Side.

National Association for Continence
PO Box 8310
Spartanburg, SC 29305
800-BLADDER (800-252-3337)
www.nafc.org

This organization is a source of education, advocacy, and support to the public and to the health professional about the causes, prevention, diagnosis, treatments, and management alternatives for incontinence.

National Cancer Institute
9000 Rockville Pike, Building 31
Bethesda, MD 20892
301-435-3848
www.cancer.gov

A division of the National Institutes of Health, the NCI is the Federal government's principal agency devoted to cancer research. There is a great deal of information about clinical trials available on the site.

National Comprehensive Cancer Network
50 Huntingdon Pike, Suite 200
Rockledge, PA 19046
888-909-NCCN (6226)
www.nccn.org

NCCN is a nonprofit corporation established in 1995 by leading cancer centers to provide up-to-date information on prevention, diagnosis, and treatment outcomes.

National Prostate Cancer Coalition
1154 15th Street NW
Washington, DC 20005
888-245-9455
www.4npcc.org

This Washington, D.C.-based advocacy organization is dedicated to pressing the federal government for increased funding of all activities in the area of prostate cancer.

Partin Tables

The Partin Tables are one tool that doctors and patients may use in making a treatment choice. The online version of the Partin Tables is at http://urology.jhu.edu/Partin_tables. By entering the PSA, Gleason score, and staging information, a probability is calculated for organ confined disease, extraprostatic extension, seminal vesicle invasion, and invasion into the lymph nodes.

www.Phoenix5.org

Phoenix5 is a nonprofit organization whose sole work is a website to help men and their companions deal with the social, emotional, and sexual issues that may come with the diagnosis of prostate cancer. It was founded in 2000 by a prostate cancer patient and contains first-person accounts of men—and their mates—who are struggling with prostate cancer.

Pro-Qura
1101 Madison Street, Suite 1170
Seattle, WA 98104
206-215-2470
www.proqura.com

Pro-Qura is a quality assurance program which exists to ensure prostate cancer patients excellent care and a higher quality of life. Pro-Qura accomplishes this by assisting brachytherapy teams in performing their very best each day through its quality assurance and affiliation programs.

Prostate Calculator
300 S. Jackson Street, Suite 540
Denver, CO 80209
www.prostatecalculator.org

This site is a service of the Artificial Neural Networks in Prostate Cancer Project and supplies online tools for diagnosis and prognosis-based systems of artificial intelligence.

Prostate Cancer Education Council

5299 DTC Boulevard, Suite 345
Greenwood Village, CO 80111
866-477-6788
www.pcaw.com

PCEC is the organization that coordinates the annual Prostate Cancer Education Awareness Week. This event offers free or low-cost prostate cancer screenings across the nation and educates men (and their mates) about the importance of early detection.

Prostate Cancer Resource Network

2803 Fruitville Road
Sarasota, FL 34237
800-915-1001
www.pcrn.org

The Prostate Cancer Resource Network is a charitable foundation dedicated to providing information, hope, and encouragement to prostate cancer patients and their families.

Radiation Therapy Oncology Group (RTOG)

1101 Market Street, 14th Floor
Philadelphia, PA 19107
215-574-3189
www.rtog.org

RTOG is a national cancer research organization that is funded by the National Cancer Institute. More than 250 medical facilities from the United States and Canada make up the RTOG. The goal of the organization is to increase survival and quality of life for people diagnosed with cancer. The RTOG contains a great deal of clinical trial information.

SeedPods

www.prostatepointers.org/seedpods

An excellent source of information on radioactive seed implants for the treatment of prostate cancer.

Side by Side

See Man to Man

Swedish Cancer Institute at Swedish Medical Center
1221 Madison Street
Seattle, WA 98104
206-386-2323 or 800-SWEDISH (800-793-3474)
www.swedish.org

The Swedish Cancer Institute is the largest cancer treatment program in the Pacific Northwest, offering a wide range of advanced cancer treatment options backed by extensive diagnostic capabilities, patient education, and support group services.

Us Too International
5003 Fairview Avenue
Downers Grove, IL 60515
800-808-7866
www.ustoo.org

Us Too is an independent network of support groups for men with prostate cancer and their families. In addition to information on local chapters, the site offers a variety of services including publications, reports on clinical trials, a calendar of events, and other useful features.

WellnessBooks.com
www.wellnessbooks.com/prostatecancer

WellnessBooks, an affiliate of Amazon.com, lists many books on prostate cancer. Read reviews submitted by readers, write reviews, and purchase the books online.

Notes

1. Wilt, T. J., et al. "Saw palmetto extracts for treatment of benign prostatic hyperplasia: a systematic review," 1998, *Journal of the American Medical Association* 280(18): 1604–09.
2. Bairati, I., et al. "Dietary fat and advanced prostate cancer," 1998, *Journal of Urology* 159(4): 1271–1275.
3. Demark-Wahnefried, W., et al. "Pilot study of dietary fat restriction and flaxseed supplementation in men with prostate cancer before surgery: exploring the effects on hormonal levels, prostate-specific antigen, and histopathologic features," 2001, *Urology* 58(1): 47–52.
4. Lu-Yao, G. L., and S. L Yao. "Population-based study of long-term survival in patient with clinically localized prostate cancer," 1997, *Lancet* 349(9056): 906–910.
5. Potosky, Arnold L., et al. "Prostate cancer practice patterns and quality of life: the prostate cancer outcomes study," October 1999, *Journal of the National Cancer Institute* 91(20): 1719–1724.
6. Catalona, W. J. "Management of cancer of the prostate," 1994, *New England Journal of Medicine* 331: 996–1004.
7. Lu-Yao, G. L., et al. "Effect of age and surgical approach on complications and short-term mortality after radical prostatectomy—a population-based study," 1999, *Urology* 54: 301–307.
8. Siegel, T., et al. "The development of erectile dysfunction in men treated for prostate cancer," 2001, *Journal of Urology*, 165(2): 430–435.

9. Talcott, James A., et al. "Patient-reported impotence and inconti-
    nence after nerve-sparing radical prostatectomy," 1997, *Journal of the
    National Cancer Institute* 89(5): 1117–1123.

10. American Cancer Society (ACS), *Chapter 108: Neoplasms of the
    Prostate*, p. 1569. Atlanta, GA.
    www.cancer.org/downloads/PUB/DOCS/SECTION30/108.pdf

11. Potosky, Arnold L., et al. "Health outcomes after prostatectomy or
    radiotherapy for prostate cancer: results from the prostate cancer out-
    comes study," 2000, *Journal of the National Cancer Institute* 92(19):
    1582–1892.

12. Zelefsky, M. J., et al. "High-dose intensity modulated radiation ther-
    apy for prostate cancer: early toxicity and biochemical outcome in
    772 patients," 2000, *International Journal of Radiation, Oncology,
    Biology, Physics.* 53(5): 1111–16.

13. Crook, Juanita, et al. "Factors influencing risk of acute urinary reten-
    tion after TRUS-guided permanent seed implantation," 2002, *Inter-
    national Journal of Radiation Oncology Biology Physics* 52(2): 453–460.

14. Pound, C. R., et al. "Natural history of progression after PSA eleva-
    tion following radical prostatectomy," 1999, *Journal of the American
    Medical Association* 281(17): 1591–1597.

15. The SPIRIT trial is comparing the results of permanent seed
    implantation and radical prostatectomy. Patients are randomized to
    receive either surgery or implantation. A willingness to cooperate in
    this trial will contribute to a better understanding of these treatments.
    For an educational video or brochure, contact Tracy Kerby, kerby001
    @surgerytrials.duke.edu, or find a video online at www.brachy4u.ca.

16. There are many companies that sell seeds including Amersham, Bard,
    Theragenics, Mentor, North American Scientific, IBt, SourceTech
    Medical, Best Medical International, IsoAid, and Implant Sciences.
    Providing this list in no way implies we suggest contacting them for a
    list of physicians doing prostate brachytherapy.

17. Note from the editors at Seattle Prostate Institute: Pro-Qura is an
    example of an external quality assurance firm. It was founded by the
    physicians of the Seattle Prostate Institute. Its goal is to enable every
    man to receive high quality seed implants no matter where he lives. For
    a physician to become an affiliate of Pro-Qura, he or she must send all
    the postimplant CT scans to the Pro-Qura staff for detailed analysis.

About the
Seattle Prostate Institute

THE SEATTLE PROSTATE INSTITUTE (SPI) was established in 1997 by a group of physicians who, in the mid-1980s, had pioneered the introduction and development of ultrasound-guided prostate implantation in the United States from their base at Seattle's Northwest Hospital. After relocating to Swedish Medical Center, another of Seattle's premier institutions, these physicians sought to expand and improve upon the work they had started with an emphasis on the highest standards of patient care, medical research, and clinical education. Seattle Prostate Institute physicians have performed thousands of prostate implants. Of the patients treated at SPI, half have come from other states and other countries in order to benefit from the expertise that has been developed in Seattle. Visit SPI's website at www.seattleprostate.com.

Editors

Peter D. Grimm, D.O.
Director, Seattle Prostate Institute
Dr. Grimm was among the first physicians in the United States to perform radioactive seed implantation for prostate cancer. He has become highly

regarded for bringing about improvements in many aspects of the procedure, and his endeavors have led to advances in technique and overall quality assurance. Dr. Grimm was instrumental in creating the SPI, and he has treated more than 2,500 patients. Along with his colleagues at SPI, he has published extensively on permanent seed implantation. He and his colleagues have trained more than 4,500 physicians, nurses, and physicists in permanent seed implantation. He is the chief executive officer of Pro-Qura, the largest internationally recognized seed implantation quality assessment company.

John C. Blasko, M.D.
Medical Director, Seattle Prostate Institute

Dr. Blasko was the first radiation oncologist to perform a perineal template and ultrasound-guided prostate implant in the United States. In 2002, the American Brachytherapy Society awarded him the Henschke Medal for outstanding contributions to the field of brachytherapy. Dr. Blasko has also been listed in *The Best Doctors in America* for several years. He has served as an officer of, and on numerous committees for, the American College of Radiology, the American Brachytherapy Society, and the National Cancer Institute. Dr. Blasko is a highly sought-after national and international speaker and has published more than 30 articles on prostate brachytherapy. He currently is the medical director of the Seattle Prostate Institute.

John E. Sylvester, M.D.
Director of Education, Seattle Prostate Institute

Dr. Sylvester is a leading expert in implant training and the use of hormonal therapy. Besides performing more than 1,200 prostate seed implantations during the past decade, he has developed several critical technical improvements in the procedure. As an internationally recognized expert in the treatment of prostate cancer, he is asked to lecture and train physicians at the top prostate cancer meetings each year. Dr. Sylvester was also the first physician in the United States to use the newest generation of radioactive seeds, and he is widely published in medical journals and textbooks. He currently directs the many physician education programs of SPI.

Maribeth Stephens
IMC Writing, LLC
Seattle, WA
www.imcwriting.biz

Ms. Stephens has more than 20 years of professional writing experience. Besides serving as writer and associate editor for *The Prostate Cancer Treatment Book*, her work has appeared nationally, regionally, and locally in a variety of media—radio, television, trade magazines, and books.

Contributors

David C. Beyer, M.D., F.A.C.R.
Arizona Oncology Services and Clinical Lecturer
University of Arizona
Phoenix, AZ

Daniel H. Clarke, M.D.
Director of Brachytherapy
Inova Alexandria Cancer Center
Alexandria, VA
www.nvro.com

Brian J. Davis, M.D., Ph.D.
Assistant Professor of Oncology
Mayo Medical School Consultant, Division of Radiation Oncology
Mayo Clinic and Foundation
Rochester, MN
www.mayoclinic.org/prostatecancer-rst.index.html

Jay Friedland, M.D.
Department of Radiation Oncology
University Community Hospital
Tampa, FL
www.uch.org/coe_cancer.asp

Celestia S. Higano, M.D.
Associate Professor
Departments of Medicine and Urology
University of Washington
Seattle, WA
http://depts.washington.edu/guoncres

Deborah A. Kuban, M.D.
Professor of Radiation Oncology
Genito-Urinary Section Chief
The University of Texas M. D. Anderson Cancer Center
Houston, TX
www.mdanderson.org

W. Robert Lee, M.D., M.S.
Associate Professor and Vice-Chairman
Department of Radiation Oncology
Wake Forest University School of Medicine
Winston-Salem, NC
www.wfubmc.edu

Gregory S. Merrick, M.D.
Schiffler Cancer Center
Wheeling Hospital and Wheeling Jesuit University
Wheeling, WV
www.wheelinghospital.com

Jeff M. Michalski, M.D., M.B.A.
Clinical Director
Associate Professor, Department of Radiation Oncology
Washington University School of Medicine
St. Louis, MO
http://radonc.wustl.edu

Brian J. Moran, M.D.
Medical Director, Chicago Prostate Cancer Center
Westmont, IL
www.prostateimplant.com

Mark A. Moyad, M.D., M.P.H.
Phil F. Jenkins Director of Complementary/Alternative Medicine
University of Michigan Medical Center—Department of Urology
Ann Arbor, MI
www.cancer.med.umich.edu/prostcan/prosintro.htm

John P. Mulhall, M.D.
Associate Professor
Director, Sexual Medicine Programs
Departments of Urology
Weill Medical College of Cornell University
New York Presbyterian Hospital and Memorial Sloan-Kettering Cancer Center
New York, NY
www.cornellurology.com/uro/cornell/sexualmedicine

Bradley R. Prestidge, M.D.
Medical Director, Texas Prostate Brachytherapy Services
Cancer Therapy and Research Center
San Antonio, TX
www.texasprostate.com

Mack Roach III, M.D.
Professor, Radiation Oncology and Urology
University of California–San Francisco
http://urology.ucsf.edu

Katsuto Shinohara, M.D.
Associate Professor, Urology
University of California–San Francisco
San Francisco, CA
http://urology.ucsf.edu

Ian M. Thompson, M.D.
Professor and Chief
Division of Urology
University of Texas Health Science Center at San Antonio
San Antonio, TX
http://urology.uthscsa.edu

J. Brantley Thrasher, M.D., F.A.C.S.
William L. Valk Distinguished Professor
Chair of Urology
University of Kansas Medical Center
Kansas City, KS
www.kumc.edu/urology

Anthony L. Zietman, M.D., M.R.C.P., F.R.C.R.
Professor, Department of Radiation Oncology
Harvard Medical School
Director of Education
Department of Radiation Oncology
Massachusetts General Hospital
Boston, MA
www.partners.org

Index

prostatectomy, 75–92
watchful waiting, 69–74
TURP (transurethral resection of the
 prostate)
defined, 10–11
external beam radiation therapy and,
 106
seed implantation and, 124, 146

Ultrasound
cancer detection and, 52–53
for pubic arch evaluation, 124,
 125–26
Urethra, 4, 6, 7
Urinary problems
AUA Symptom Score Sheet for, 121,
 122
brachytherapy and, 121, 134, 140–47,
 182–83
catheters, 182–83
as common side effect, 70
external radiation and, 109–10
prostatectomy and, 90–91
radiation therapy and, 106
Urothelial cell carcinoma (UCC), 13

Vacuum erection devices (VEDs), 89
Vas deferens, 4, 5, 6
Velban (vinblastine), 173
Vepsid (etoposide), 173

Viagra, 86, 88–89, 98, 109, 110, 118,
 138, 149
Vitamin C, 142, 143
Vitamin D, 31, 32
Vitamin E, 24–25
Vitamin K, 33

Watchful waiting
as active surveillance, 70
advantages of, 73, 193
candidates for, 70–72
defined, 69
disadvantages of, 73
examinations during, 73
PSA levels and, 72, 73–74
for recurrent cancer, 170–71
survival statistics, 69
Watson, Davis, 87
Weight gain, 28, 164
Weight loss
low-carbohydrate diets and, 35–36
momentum effect and, 33–34
for prostate health, 34
saturated fat and, 27–28
"What-if" thinking, 62

Young, Dr. Hugh Hampton, 75

Zoledronic acid (Zometa), 174
Zones, prostate, 4–5